Breaking the Ice

The Story of
Helen Blanchard, DTM
the First Woman President of
Toastmasters International

Helen Blanchard

with Deanne Durrett

Dedicated to
Toastmasters International
The program that changes lives — it did mine.

HBlanchard Enterprises
San Diego, California

Breaking the Ice: The Story of Helen Blanchard, DTM, the First Woman President of Toastmasters International

For information:

HBlanchard Enterprises
P. O. Box 60203
San Diego, California 92166

ISBN: 978-0-9816640-1-9
LCCN 2008907100

Author photo by CeCe Canton, 2008
Interior and cover design and layout by Robert Goodman, Silvercat™, San Diego, California <www.silvercat.com>

Printed in the United States of America

Contents

Acknowledgements

Thank you to my many friends who gave me the encouragement that made this book a reality. I wish I could name all of you, but although that is not possible, there are those whose contribution call for special mention:

Deanne Durrett who "saw" a book in my life and worked with me to put it into print;

Sheryl Roush not only for her interest and direction, but for sharing her valuable knowledge about publishing;.

Chuck Borough for his guidance and counsel;

Beth Black who edited with extraordinary thoughtfulness and concern;

Dee Dees for support , sharing, and caring;

and Jim Tucker who was always there with stellar advice.

Chapter 1

"Homer"

JOIN TOASTMASTERS AND PRESENT WITH CONFIDENCE the headline claimed. Confidence! The word leaped off the page. That was exactly what I needed. I had been given an assignment that punched a hole and pushed me through that once-solid barrier between man's work and woman's work.

It was 1970. I worked for the United States Navy Research and Development Center in San Diego, California. Until that time, I had worked at typical female jobs, but in my new position, I would travel to offshore Navy test sites and train the engineers to use a uniform method for analyzing and reporting the technical data they collected.

The promising headline was in our Center newsletter that I was reading during lunch. I didn't read further where the smaller print limited the invitation to "Men on the Move." Instead, I saw a familiar name listed as the contact person; I called Bob Bolam right away and asked for more information about the program. He explained that Toastmasters was an all-male organization. Women didn't join Toastmasters; they joined Toastmistresses — the same type of organization but

exclusively for women. Bob suggested the possibility of starting a Toastmistress Club at the Center.

Continuing the search, I followed this conversation by making some phone calls to women I thought were "on the move."
None shared my interest in learning to "present with confidence." So, I reported my findings back to Bob, thanked him
for the suggestion, and returned to work.

In my new position, I had made several trips to test sites
at San Clemente Island off the coast of Southern California,
Hawaii, Cape Cod, Bremerton in Washington State, Andros
Island in the Bahamas and Cuba. Although I was confident in
my knowledge of the data collection methods we used, I was
walking in a highly technical man's world without the educational background of an engineering degree, which certainly
would have increased my confidence and probably would have
made my training presentations more palatable to the engineers. As it was, I felt that I had to prove myself, over and over,
and I was well acquainted with the menacing butterflies that
accompanied me to every briefing.

Although I was disappointed that there would be no help
for me, I put the matter aside and forgot about that phone conversation. Then, about three weeks later, Bob called. He told
me that he had brought up the possibility of my membership
at the last meeting and the membership had voted to accept
me in their club. As much as I needed the help Toastmasters
claimed to offer, I was quite sure that I didn't want to go to a
meeting if anyone objected. So, I asked Bob if all the members
had agreed. He said, "Helen, it was unanimous." Later, I found
out that the case for my membership in the Center's Toastmasters club had been well presented. Bob had reminded the
members that the club met on Federal land, on Federal time,
and that I was a Federal employee.

After hearing the news that I could join, I began to wonder what I had gotten myself into. I had never attended a meeting. All I knew was what I had read in the ad. I didn't know what they did. Would I like it? Would I actually benefit? I didn't know. I had asked to join and now that I was accepted, I couldn't back down graciously, so I decided to forge ahead and attend at least one meeting.

The club at the Center was a small group with about 15 members; there were about ten present that day. I knew Bob, and recognized a few other faces. Still, this was unknown territory and my senses were on the alert as I walked through the door. I detected no animosity, my tension eased, and I felt welcome.

I was impressed with the Toastmasters program from the very first meeting. I had expected to learn how to improve my speaking skills and make better presentations. However, I had not realized that another aspect of the program, the evaluation process, would be just as valuable to me. As part of my job, I reviewed and critiqued the engineer's reports from the test ranges and as I listened to the constructive evaluations intended to encourage and help the speaker improve, I knew I would benefit from this program in more ways than advertised.

Once I saw the program in action, I wanted to join. I formally applied for membership on June 2, 1970 under the non-gender-specific name of H. Blanchard. Although all membership applications are sent to International Headquarters for processing, I trusted that my membership was assured and, thus, I became an active participant in the club.

The club was having a successful membership drive with a steady flow of new members. I was one of four new members that day, and we needed to schedule our Ice Breakers right away. Because I was the only woman, the gentlemen politely allowed me to give mine first. My induction and Ice Breaker were scheduled for the next meeting and since the club met bimonthly, I had about two weeks to prepare my first speech.

(No. LSF –2927-8-70) Courtesy Space and Naval Warfare Systems San Diego

Club 2539 Administrative Vice President, Mike Pricket, presents membership pins to new members, Joe Dodds, Helen Blanchard, Hulett McDowell, and Art Donham

In this introductory speech, the new member tells the group a little about himself or herself. This is thought to be an easy subject for the first speech since it involves talking about something the speaker knows well. But I didn't find it all that easy and I worked very hard to make my speech informative and interesting; seasoned with interesting anecdotes and a touch of humor.

I was nervous when I arrived at that second meeting and seeing the program made it worse. There were three speakers scheduled for that day. One was another Ice Breaker but the third was a veteran Toastmaster — the president of the club and head of the computer department at the Navy Center. I was sure that he wasn't in the program because he needed to improve his speaking skills or gain confidence in presenting. He was an excellent speaker with a polished presentation and delivery. He was there because he was asking all his people to join Toastmasters and he was leading by example. I still remember how impressed I was by his title, "Automation and How it Affects our Lives." I definitely felt intimidated as I stood to talk about my family and work.

My evaluator said that I didn't appear nervous, though I certainly felt that way! He said he liked my use of humor but added that I needed to work on making a smoother delivery. The big eye-opener for me was the "ah" counter's evaluation. This designated person keeps track of annoying filler words that detract from the message — the "ahs" and "uhms." He said that I used so many that he just stopped counting mid-speech. I was completely unaware that I had that habit. I attributed some of this to nervousness. However, I suspected that my technical speeches were peppered with these meaningless filler words.

When the speaker awards were announced, the winner was the veteran Toastmaster but I was voted second best. I also joined the others in responding to Table Topics questions that day. I don't remember the topic but I do remember the thrill when my brief impromptu speech won a trophy that the group had dubbed the *Traveling Spark Plug*.

Several weeks later, my membership application was returned with a request for a first name. Quite sure that we shouldn't use *Helen*, the club president asked me what male name I would like to use. I had to admit I had never given that much thought — while I was mentally reviewing possible male names beginning with "H" — Herman? Harry? Harold? — another member suggested that the club name me. They did just that, devoting the Table Topics portion of the next meeting to naming H. Blanchard. Since I had already given my Ice Breaker speech, the membership had some information to use in choosing my name. The winner, Joe Dodds, wove a delightful story around my maiden name (Pallas), the fact that I enjoy poetry, and looked Grecian. He suggested that there was no better name for *Helen* — referring to Helen of Troy and the Trojan horse — than *Homer*. And I agreed. Homer, I remained until November of 1971 when World Headquarters sent word that our club at the Center — Club No. 2539 — could accept female members. The club had requested this because discrimination was not an option since we were meeting on Federal property. Thus, Helen could replace Homer on the membership rolls. This opened the door for an overall policy change in August of 1973 that made it possible for any individual club to revise its bylaws to allow women in its membership. With more women continually joining the workforce and finding opportunities for management positions, everyone benefited from making the organization coed. I had always seen the Toastmasters experience as an opportunity and set out to gain the most I could from the program.

As I worked through the projects in the Toastmasters manual, I could feel myself gaining confidence and I noticed that my speeches contained fewer and fewer of those pesky filler words. I also learned how to organize a speech and then present it using effective hand gestures, voice tone, and volume variation.

At the meetings, when my turn came to serve, I became the evaluator, "ah" counter, timer, toastmaster, grammarian and table topics master — filling whatever role our group needed to produce a fruitful meeting. While performing my assigned duties I paid particular attention to those aspects of all the speeches I heard. In the process, I learned from other's

TOASTMASTERS INTERNATIONAL

EXCEPTION TO CLUB CONSTITUTION

CLUB #___2539____

DISTRICT #___5____

In response to the club application, Article III of the Club
Constitution of the _____NEL_____
Toastmasters Club is modified to read as follows:

> "Any person of good moral character, at least
> 18 years of age, may become a member upon..."

This exception to the membership criteria, as provided for in
Article III, Section 2, of the Bylaws of Toastmasters
International, is granted pursuant to action taken by the .
Board of Directors on November 19, 1971, Santa Ana, California.
This exception is valid only for the period of time that the
basis of such exception exists.

VERIFIED BY _____
            Robert T. Buck Engle
            Executive Director
            Toastmasters International

                          Date: NOVEMBER 24, 1971

After receipt of this letter from WHQ, Helen replaced Homer on the membership roll and the door opened for an overall change in policy in 1973.

mistakes and high points almost as much as I did from the
evaluations of my own speeches.

Still, one of the biggest benefits for me came from presenting
speeches to the group on a regular basis, and I was told that
my presence changed the dynamics of the group in a positive
way. Bob, a veteran Toastmaster of about 13 years, told me that
with a woman in the audience, he experienced nervousness
while speaking for the first time in years. He went on to say
that as more women entered the workforce, men would need
to become comfortable with a coed audience.

The benefits of the Toastmasters organization have influenced almost every aspect of my life — and in return my life experiences have contributed greatly to my Toastmaster's success by providing speech material and motivation. The story of my birth foretold my future and my early years laid the foundation of my destiny.

In 1985, the famous radio personality, Paul Harvey, included a story in his show, "The Rest of the Story," that was about the election and installation of the new President of Toastmasters International: a woman who had joined the organization 15 years earlier under the assumed name of Homer. In truth there was much more to tell. For that reason, here is *the rest of my story...*

Chapter 2

Nebraska Roots

My story begins in the Midwest, in the northeastern corner of Nebraska, where the Corn Belt spreads across the heart of America. This is farm country: rolling hills blanketed by corn fields and pasture lands, dotted with rural homes and small towns. It is where, if you examine the map closely, you will find Pender, Nebraska — the place of my birth.

By sundown, May 17, 1926, Anna and Frank Pallas had a new baby in their family. I was their fourth child and the first to be born in a hospital. The fifth, my brother Earle would arrive eighteen months later. In those days, childbirth was the woman's domain and men were expected to be elsewhere during the process. After Dad brought Mom to the Pender hospital, he went home, confident that she was in good hands. Since May is one of the busiest months on the farm, he did the chores and went to the field with my older brothers, Milt, age 11 and Bill, 9, while my older sister, Vlasta, 13, took over for Mom in the house with the help of the neighbor women. So, in the first few hours of my life it was just Mom and me in the care of our family doctor and his nurse.

Blanchard Collection

When I was a little older, Dad showed me off with pride and from that time on, throughout his life, the two of us shared many special times together."

The nurse was bubbling with excitement as she laid me in my mother's arms. My hair grew in an unusual pattern, and she pointed it out. She eagerly explained that a child born with a "double crown" was destined to go overseas. I am sure my mother smiled at hearing such an amusing old wives' tale as she examined my tiny hands and feet. She may have enjoyed the dream but her heart told her that I wouldn't have that opportunity. In Nebraska farm country, a baby girl did not grow up to travel the world. The child in her arms would grow up to be a farmer's wife or maybe a teacher; few other opportunities were available to women in that time and place.

Although I am a native-born Cornhusker, my father was born in Moravia and the Pallas family heritage is Czech. Throughout history, the map of Eastern Europe has been redrawn many times. Although boundaries and rulers changed, the hearts of the people and their culture remained Czech. My Grandfather Pallas became dissatisfied with the European political climate when — under Austro-Hungarian rule — the sons of Moravia were compelled to serve a seven-year stint in the Austrian army. Like so many others of his generation, my grandfather wanted a better life and freedom. He decided to join the flow of immigrants to America when his eldest son reached 21 and my dad, the fourth from the eldest, was 15 years old.

After a long journey over land and sea, the family — with all nine children — arrived safely in New York harbor, made their way through Ellis Island in March of 1902, and continued by train until they reached Nebraska. The new arrivals stayed in Wahoo, Nebraska, with relatives until they found a home in the town of Thurston. They settled in and became United States citizens. Dad was proud to be an American and very loyal to his new homeland. Still, I think Moravia — the land of his birth — never lost its place in his heart. Through the years, he often spoke of the beautiful country he remembered from his childhood and youth.

My mother, Anna Rihanek, was born in Nebraska to Czech parents, and in the early 1900s, the Rihanek and the Pallas families were neighbors in Thurston. By the time Dad noticed Mother, her two older sisters were married and her mother had grown fatally ill. Grandmother didn't want to "go" without knowing that her youngest daughter had a secure future. Playing the role of matchmaker, she encouraged a romance between her unmarried daughter and the young Czech man next door. He was smitten but a little reluctant because of the age difference: he was a grown man at 23 and — at 14 — she was barely a teenager. Yet, eventually he made his feelings known, and Mom was flattered by the attention from the handsome older man next door. He stole her heart. Grandma lived long enough to see them married, and she went to her grave content.

I have to give Mom and Dad credit for holding our family of seven together during the Depression years. The hard times of the 1920s and 30s hit the urban areas full force and about a third of the U.S. workforce lost their jobs. We were fortunate that Dad had the foresight after the birth of his third child to move our family to the farm. He knew the livestock and land would provide food for us no matter how the national economy fared.

A typical day on the farm started with Mom in the kitchen. As the rest of the family woke and dressed, the aroma of a hearty breakfast wafted throughout the house. We began the day with grace at the breakfast table. The workday, for the men, started at dawn and ended about sundown — suppertime — most of the year. In planting season and during harvest, however, they worked as long as they had enough light. When night had fallen, we gathered again for the evening meal, and Mom's chores ended sometime after the dishes were

Mom and Dad on their wedding day in 1911.

done. When the change of seasons meant less daylight, she began and ended her day by the light of a kerosene lamp.

Every person had responsibilities — youngsters performed chores before and after school. The boys helped Dad with the livestock and crops. By the time they were 9 or 10, they were learning to plow and operate farm machinery. Some young men dropped out of school because their families needed them to work on their farms. In fact, my oldest brother Milt quit high school after his freshman year and carried a "man's load" by the time he was 15 years old.

I began helping Mom with the housework, gardening, and food preserving at a pretty early age. I can't remember when I didn't help with these chores. Later, there were times when I was needed in the field to perform one of the easier tasks. Mom insisted that I wear long-sleeved smocks, hats and gloves to protect myself from the sun when I worked outside. Summer or winter, this was an unbroken rule. Ladies didn't work in the field; tanned skin and freckles were not, as she put it, "fashionable." Of course, I wanted to be fashionable with a city-girl complexion, so whenever I could sneak some time for pampering, I gave myself a facial with milk.

Sometimes, the cattle were put out to graze in an area bordering the corn field. On these days, it was my job to keep the cattle out of the corn. I suffered through this job on horseback, detesting every minute of it. Our horses were not ponies for riding. They were huge work horses, with extremely wide backs and each with a very stubborn will. Every horse was trained to move slowly in a straight line harnessed to a plow. When I rode one, I needed it to turn quickly and trot. This huge, stubborn animal usually ignored the pull on the reins and responded to the jabs of my heel with a snort. On hot summer days, this job reduced me to tears more often than not. This was my most dangerous task. However, it posed little threat compared to that faced by the men and boys on the farm.

When operating dangerous farm equipment and machinery, just one small slip-up can result in a tragic accident. Milt lost some toes from his right foot in a saw mishap and Earle lost all his fingers in a corn-picking machine when he was just 20 years old. When he was 40, another farm accident took his life.

That old saying: "A man works from sun to sun but a woman's work is never done" certainly applies to farm life. When I think of all Mom did on that farm, I'm astonished that she didn't collapse from sheer exhaustion. She prepared everything we ate from scratch, three hearty meals every day, cooked on a wood-burning stove with no temperature gage. When she wasn't in the kitchen, Mom tended the garden and the poultry, did the laundry in a hand-operated wringer-washing machine and ironed with a flat iron that she'd heated on the stove. Throughout the summer she canned farm produce (vegetables, fruit, and meat) in Mason jars and stored the winter's supply of food in the cellar. She gathered the eggs, helped with the milking, and separated the cream. On Saturdays she took the extra eggs and cream to market and used the money to buy sugar, flour, coffee and other items the farm didn't produce.

We attended church every week and afterward Mom prepared Sunday dinner. Once the dishes were done, she relaxed for awhile. This is the only time I remember seeing my mother sit down to rest. Monday morning she was first to rise and ready to begin her new workweek. While I was growing up, I worked at her side. Mom never took the time to teach me (or Vlasta) to cook. She was always too busy to let Sis or me fiddle around in the kitchen. She always said, "I never worry about you girls learning to cook since you enjoy eating so much." She was right!

Throughout the week, Mom spent many hours seated at the Singer sewing machine with her feet rocking the treadle. She made almost everything we wore. Sometimes she used new fabric but most of time she recycled hand-me-downs, updating the style and altering the size. This was the way it was for most farm families if they were blessed with a good wife and mother as we were. I appreciated Mom's skill and effort but in my teen years, I longed for things like a new winter coat: ready-made and mine alone. I knew that if I stayed on the farm I would follow my mother's footsteps to a hard life with little cash. Therefore, I vowed that once I became an adult, I'd never live on a farm.

Mom and Dad had a good marriage despite the hardships, and they were able to celebrate their 56th wedding anniversary. A year later, at age 70, Mom was killed in an automobile accident.

Four years later, when Dad was 83, he grew close to Irene Berner, a widow who had attended church with my parents for years. Irene became the second Mrs. Frank Pallas. She shared Dad's golden years and became a beloved member of our family.

I attended school in a one-room schoolhouse located about a quarter mile from our front door and so I wasn't required to make any of those notoriously arduous walks to school that many Midwesterners describe to their children. Still, Northeastern Nebraska winters are often brutal, with deep snow and howling winds. I remember one year, Dad and the boys made a path from the house to the barn through drifts that had to be six to eight foot high.

In those days, snow was not considered a reason to cancel school. If the teacher could get to school, any student who didn't make it was counted absent — and, our teacher was always there! When bad weather was predicted and expected to make the roads impassable, the teacher spent the night at our house and walked the quarter mile in the morning.

When the teacher stayed over, we put her in my room and I slept in a very small room off my parent's bedroom — I think it was meant to be a large closet. I didn't mind giving up my room; I liked having Teacher in our home. In fact, I thought it was pretty neat. I would watch her as she sat at our kitchen table, grading papers and working on her lesson plans. In my daydreams, I imagined myself as a teacher, handling the same duties. By this time, Vlasta was teaching and since I was sure I didn't want to be a farm wife, I decided that I would be a teacher, too.

I enjoyed learning and became an avid reader. I looked forward to Art class on Friday afternoon when we could bring out the crayons, paste and scissors. Most of the time, we were given a project to color; pictures our teacher reproduced. I kept the assignments I especially liked, planning to give them to my own students, someday. I was always sad when the school year ended in spring and eager for the next session to begin in the fall.

A dedicated student, I took advantage of an opportunity that was unique in the one-room school: after finishing their schoolwork, the younger students could listen in on the upper-grade lessons. In those days, students were allowed to progress at their own pace and I skipped ahead two grades. This gave me an advantage scholastically but proved to be a big disadvantage socially. In years to come, I would remember my elementary school days as a joy and my biggest misery.

The combination of home visits by the teacher and my fast track education earned me a "Teacher's Pet" label. The resulting treatment I received from my classmates during recesses and lunch was not fun. I was teased and excluded from games that the teacher didn't supervise. In other words, when the kids chose sides, I was left out. More than anything, I wanted to be accepted. I thought that the other children would play with me if I didn't do so well, so I cheated on a test — deliberately failing. The teacher knew something was wrong and tested me orally the next day. I forgot the answers I had given on the written exam and the correct answers just popped out. After that little misadventure, I continued my elementary education on the fast track and endured the misery of recess. I passed the state exam and graduated from the eighth grade. The next fall, I enrolled in Pender High School. I was 11 years old.

There were no extra curricular activities beyond recess and the hour-long lunch break at the one-room school house. However, when I went to high school, I had the opportunity to choose one extra curricular activity. My first choice was chorus. At the end of the second session, the teacher asked me to stay after class. He was gentle and apologetic when he said, "I'm sorry, Helen. You're a nice girl but you can't sing." Then he went on to offer me some encouragement. "You're tall; I suggest you join the basketball team for your extra activity." So, I did and I was welcomed on the team where I played jump center during my two years at Pender High School.

Sometime after my transfer from chorus to basketball, our minister asked me to join the choir and I told him about my failure in singing. After a brief pause for thought, he asked me to fill a chair in the choir and... not sing! Thus, I became a member of the church choir but never sang a note. Sitting in the congregation, my mother proudly watched me mouth the words. When my lips slipped out of sync she would shake her head and frown.

In Nebraska at the time, a high school graduate with two years of a process called Normal Training could teach in a one-room schoolhouse after passing the rigorous State exams. This is what I wanted to do. However, I would have to go to Wisner High School for Normal Training. Wisner was about twice as far from our home as Pender. My parents could not afford daily transportation to Wisner or room and board for me so we looked for a family that would let me do household chores for my keep.

They interviewed a couple with three daughters and were satisfied that all would be well before they arranged for my room and board. I lived with the Harris family (name changed to protect their privacy) throughout the school year and visited my own family every other weekend. Although the Harris' considered my work payment enough for my room and board, my parents considered their hospitality a favor and Mom sent them butter, eggs, cream, and fresh meat when we butchered.

Mr. Harris was as protective of me as he was his own daughters. In his fatherly role, he always wanted to know where I was going, with whom, and he set the time that I was expected home.

In the middle of my junior year, a new boy came to school. He was from California and had a car. He was nice looking, too. It was a big deal for me when he sat by me in study hall: California, cute boy, *and . . . a car!* It became really big when he asked me — a 14 year old junior — to the senior prom. I had to tell him that I was expected to visit my parents on the farm that weekend. He said it didn't matter and he would take me to the farm after the dance. What could I say but Yes!

Mr. Harris insisted on having a "little talk" with my date before the prom, which took place before I came downstairs. And when I came down to greet my date, everything seemed fine. We went to the prom, had a good time, and as he promised, he drove me to the farm after the dance.

When we arrived, I thought he would walk me to the door. Of course, I was wondering if he would try to kiss me and what I should do. Instead, he almost shouted, "Good night!" while I climbed out of the car. His tires spewed gravel as he sped away into the night. He didn't sit by me in study hall again. The Golden Boy graduated and went back to California. Later, I found out that Mr. Harris had told my young man that my father was very protective; he had a shot gun and wouldn't hesitate to use it if he thought someone was "messing" with his daughter.

I graduated from high school in May of the next year and that same month I celebrated my 16th birthday. My grade point average made me eligible for a scholarship from the State of Nebraska for tuition at Wayne's State Teacher's College. However, I was anxious to teach and I wanted that new coat! So with my diploma and the results of the State Exam tucked in my purse, I went about applying for a position as a *teacher*.

Chapter 3

The War Years

In the fall of 1942, the rumblings of World War II had risen to a full roar. I began teaching in a one-room school as the nation's young men were joining the service, struggling through boot camp and shipping out. Thus, this terrible war and America's massive effort to prevail framed the backdrop for my life as a young single woman.

Under usual circumstances a sixteen year old was considered too young to teach, even in a one-room rural school. However, I was tall and mature for my age. The school board members who interviewed me assumed that I was the usual 18 or 19 year old graduating from high school. To my delight, I was hired and assigned to a one room school about 15 miles from the farm. Transportation would have been a problem if not for my brother, Earle. He was now attending Wisner High School and had purchased an old car with the profits from a calf he raised as a 4-H project. Since he passed by my school on his way to Wisner, we easily reached an agreement that provided transportation for me and gas money for him.

The job paid $60 a month, more than I had expected and a pretty good salary in 1942 rural America. When I received my first check, I began paying my parents $20 a month for my room and board and I bought my long-desired new coat. It was blue tweed with the warmth of wool: the latest fashion, my size and my style. I loved it!

I taught in a typical one-room school house — a small white building with the identifying bell tower over the front door. It housed about 30 desks with a few to spare after my 24 students, in grades one through eight, were seated and ready for class. Most schools were heated by a wood-burning pot-bellied stove but mine was more modern with a coal bin and a furnace in the basement. Our view outside, however, leaned toward the rural, presenting a water pump and outhouses.

The teacher (usually female in these rural schools) performed all sorts of schoolhouse duties. She was the playground supervisor, janitor, nurse and disciplinarian. To accomplish all this, I arrived early each morning. During the winter months — which was most of the school year — I scooped coal and started the furnace. I pumped fresh drinking water from the well and on most winter days, I shoveled snow and ice from the walks and steps. In the midst of performing these tasks, I rang the warning bell at seven thirty and the final bell at eight o'clock, when school began. The school day ended at four o'clock, and I tidied up the room. Then I rode home with Earle and by the time we arrived, Mom had supper waiting for us. After the dishes were done, I sat at the table, grading papers and preparing for the next day as I had seen my teacher do several years earlier. It seemed I had come full circle and my dream had been fulfilled.

Most of my students earned good grades and seemed to enjoy school. I was particularly fond of one girl who reminded me so much of myself at her age. She was enthusiastic, with a desire to please. While this child was a joy to teach, I had others

I bought my long-desired new coat when I received my first paycheck. I was 16 and quite proud!

who presented more of a challenge. One 15-year-old boy in the eighth grade had missed some school due to illness. Catching up proved to be too difficult and he had failed the state test required for graduation — twice. Once he reached sixteen, by state law, his chance for further education would end unless he passed the test. He would be too old for grade school and couldn't go on to high school. I helped him as much as I could that year, and he worked hard. Our effort paid off and he passed the State exam in the spring. This was a high-note of my teaching career. Nevertheless, these joys were not enough to sustain me, and my days in this profession were growing short.

Young and idealistic, I thought all students adored their teachers and each came with a set of appreciative parents. I did enjoy polished apples on my desk in fall and bouquets of wild flowers in spring. However, there was a behind-the-scenes aspect of being "Teacher" that I had not witnessed — parents can be difficult. I soon found out that several of my students were cousins, the children of siblings who liked to feud. During an outbreak of this sibling rivalry, one parent would send a note instructing me to keep their children from playing with the other cousins. Sometimes I was even asked to hold one child after school so he or she wouldn't walk home with the others. When I didn't follow these instructions — it didn't seem right for me to discipline children who were behaving well at school — I would be visited by an angry parent. These after-school reproaches happened so often that I dreaded the end of each day. I grew disillusioned by midyear and was ready to quit. Mom, however, was determined to see me continue. She insisted, "When you obligate yourself to do a job, you must do your best and finish the task."

My mother and I made a visit to the president of the school board. He must have contacted the feuding families — or maybe

Blanchard Collection

I thoroughly enjoyed the classroom and my students; however, dealing with some difficult parents influenced my decision to leave the teaching profession the next year.

they found some Christmas spirit. Whatever the reason, the sibling rivalry quieted down for awhile after the first of the year. Unfortunately, it returned with a vengeance in the spring. As it turned out, my school district was known for its difficult parents, and this particular family had a notorious reputation. Experienced teachers had refused to teach at my school. Learning this confirmed for me the reason they paid me more than expected and hired me without asking my age.

In later years when I looked back at this time in my life for speech material, I have always blamed my decision to leave the teaching profession on the "feuding family ordeal." But now, as I rediscover the heart of that sixteen-year-old girl, I realize she needed more social activities, fun…and boys. My dating prospects were limited to about three young men: a farm boy who had not gone off to war because of a heart condition and two young servicemen when they were home on leave. I visited girlfriends occasionally and attended church with my parents. However, all this added together didn't make much of a social life for a young woman who was about to turn seventeen.

That spring I signed a contract to teach at another school and I had the usual three month summer break before classes began in the fall. When Milt and Florence, his wife, invited me to visit them in Waukegan, Illinois — almost next door to the Great Lakes Naval Training Center — I jumped at the chance. World War II was raging across Europe and the Pacific. And as America's young men were called into military service, just about all of them passed through military training centers. There was one thing I knew that summer: I wanted to be where the boys were.

I had stayed with Milt and Florence the preceding summer to help out after their baby, Bobby, was born. So I felt at home when I returned for a visit in the summer of 1943. Like most young couples at the time, their home was small and lacked a guest room. Since I intended only a short visit, we tossed the couch cushions on the floor and that was where I slept.

I don't remember facing any dire need for money that summer. But I began searching for work almost immediately and landed a job in the accounting department at Abbott Laboratories, the pharmaceutical firm. No previous experience was required and new employees were trained on the job. Working in a group of about 10 women, I quickly learned to sort, alphabetize and tally the receipts from Abbott's drugstore customers across the country. By the end of the summer, I was promoted to supervisor of my unit and received an attractive raise.

After considering those experiences with the feuding parents as opposed to the lure of more money at Abbott Laboratories

Blanchard Collection

I visited my brother Milt, Florence, and Bobby the summer after my school-marm experience. As it turned out, I found a job in Waukegan and made my home with them for the next two years

and the young men at the Naval Training Center, I wrote to cancel the school contract. When I heard a replacement was found — my teaching days were over.

I often wonder how my life would have been had I continued teaching. Our children are our future and to have an impact on them in their formative years is a service that cannot be underestimated. However, I know that this profession was not the path to my destiny. Still, that year as a teacher contributed to the person I became, and I wouldn't trade anything for that experience.

At Abbott Laboratories, I received on-the-job training throughout the accounting department. After I had been there about a year, I began filling in at the bookkeeping machine when an operator was absent. Once I acquired the necessary speed and accuracy, and there was an opening, I was promoted to bookkeeping machine operator. This was the "top of the line position" in that department with pretty good pay.

The frigid winter weather on the shore of Lake Michigan helped me to realize that I needed something more shielding than my beloved blue tweed wool coat. I began dreaming about the cozy warmth of fur. Of course my salary at Abbott's couldn't begin to pay for a fur coat so I took a second job working at a diner. I worked four-hour shifts, waiting tables at this "greasy spoon" until I earned enough to buy my coat.

While I lived with Milt and Florence, I enjoyed being with them and I didn't mind the streetcar ride from their place to work. But my visit had developed into something that lasted much longer than originally planned. After a couple of years, I was ready to be on my own and welcomed the opportunity to share an apartment with a coworker and her young daughter. Besides having a room of my own with a regular bed, I could avoid the streetcar ride and simply walk to work. As soon as I was able, I purchased that fur coat and walking in the chilly weather became much more tolerable. This was a wonderful accomplishment for me, but there were other hardships during this time.

As long as I'd lived on the farm, rationing hadn't carried much of an impact on my life. However, Americans everywhere were constantly aware of the war and greatly affected by the Japanese attack on the United States — December 7, 1941. People of my generation know exactly where we were and what we were doing when we heard the news that would bring the United States into World War II. I was just 15, a few months shy of high school graduation. Dad was driving me back to Wisner that Sunday afternoon. We were listening to the car radio when the news hit the airways that Japan had bombed Pearl Harbor. We were stunned. How could this happen? A vast ocean protected the United States from foreign enemies. Several moments passed as we sat in silence. I don't remember who spoke first or what was said. This was a huge event; we were under attack! Would they strike again? How soon? Where? Being with Dad gave me some sense of security. When we arrived at the Harris's home, I didn't want to stay and I knew Dad didn't want to leave me.

The next day at school, the students and staff gathered in the auditorium and we listened to President Roosevelt's speech asking Congress to declare war on Japan. He began the speech with words I have never forgotten: "Yesterday, December 7, 1941 — a date which will live in infamy –" Shortly after declaring war on Japan, Congress declared war on Germany.

By this time, German forces were advancing across Europe and many of America's young men were ready to fight for European freedom. My brother Bill was already serving in the U.S.

Blanchard Collection

In May 1942, my brother Bill was serving in the U.S. Army/Air Force. We posed for this photo when he came home on leave.

Army/Air Force, and Milt had tried to enlist but didn't pass the physical because of his missing toes. While the young men went off to war, some American women kept the home fires burning for America's children while others filled vacancies left in the workforce. Still others marched off to newly created factory jobs that processed food for the troops and supplied them with clothing, medical supplies, arms and ammunition.

When I moved to Waukegan, the civilian sacrifices of war became a reality. Fresh meat, so plentiful on the farm, was now extremely scarce. When it was available, it took too many ration stamps to be affordable. Meat was being shipped overseas to feed the troops and civilians were encouraged to eat canned Spam. (Along with most people who remember the War Years, I hate Spam!) Everything needed to supply the troops was in short supply on the home front. Items that everyone considered essential were rationed — including sugar, coffee, butter, shoes, gasoline and tires. Other items such as silk stockings and cigarettes were scarce and sold on a first-come; first-served basis. People stood in long lines to buy rationed or scarce items when they became available. Whenever I saw a line, I stepped in without knowing what was being sold. If the supply lasted long enough, I bought the scarce item. If I didn't need it, Milt, Florence, or the baby did.

Rationed gasoline and tires made travel difficult. I think Milt must have saved gasoline coupons for months to buy fuel for a trip to visit our family in Pender. There were no *Golden Arches* along America's highways back then, so Florence made sandwiches for the trip — meat sandwiches! We hadn't seen roast beef in the market for months. While we were eating, and I was enjoying the unusual sweet taste of this meat, Florence admitted that she had gone to a market in Milwaukee that sold horse meat. I stopped chewing and couldn't swallow. My stomach began to churn. I am not sure what happened next, but the memory leading to that moment has stayed with me.

Back then, every woman loved sheer stockings. When Japan stopped shipping silk to the United States, nylon hose replaced silk stockings. Then, nylon was needed for parachutes, so stockings of any kind became very scarce. We women willingly sacrificed to support the troops but refused to abandon fashion. We made do with leg make-up and even used our eyebrow pencils to draw counterfeit stocking seams up the backs of our legs. Although many items were in short supply, our country was united on the home front. I never heard of a single anti-war protest. In fact, the mood of the Midwest — and I think the entire nation — was total commitment to do whatever was needed to win the war. I think we all realized our freedom was at stake and it was a do or die situation.

Every city near a military base had at least one USO Club where young servicemen could come to socialize and relax, meet local girls, talk and dance. I volunteered to work at a local USO club. The volunteers served as hostesses and dance partners. It was a clean environment with chaperones and no alcohol. We weren't allowed to leave the club with a serviceman. However, there were no rules against accepting a date that didn't originate at the club.

My life in Waukegan was fairly routine from 1943 to 1946. But two major events during that time held a tremendous impact on all our lives: President Roosevelt's death and the end of the war.

When I left work and walked into the street on April 12, 1945, most people I met were crying. I couldn't imagine why. Then, I heard someone say that President Roosevelt had died and, of course, my eyes filled with tears, as well. Franklin Delano Roosevelt had been elected to a fourth term in office and he was loved by the majority of American people. When I mention Roosevelt's death in my speeches, I always say that I was not only crying because Roosevelt had died; I was also crying because Harry Truman would now be president. The Country was still at war and there didn't seem to be a lot of confidence in Truman — at least no one I knew thought much of him or his leadership capabilities. Roosevelt had been at the helm during a difficult economic recovery and enjoyed the confidence of a majority of the American people as a war president; his shoes were hard to fill.

A second date I will never forget is August 15, 1945. I'd gone to a movie, and in the middle of the feature the film stopped. The lights came on. I could hear people shouting outside. I ran outside the theater and stepped into an enormous celebration. People were just going crazy. I soon realized that the war was over! I edged my way through the crowd toward the street-car stop. Then I discovered that the streetcars weren't running — no vehicles could move through the swarm of people in the street. Would I ever make it home? It didn't matter. I joined the celebration.

The war was over and the boys would be coming home. One would be a very special young Navy Chief Petty Officer. He served aboard the Casablanca class escort carrier, USS Kasaan Bay (CVE 69), during the invasion of Southern France, and his ship was then sent to the Pacific. In later years, I felt glad that I didn't know John Blanchard during the war — it would have been so hard, knowing that he was in harm's way.

Chapter 4

Navy Wife

In November 1945, a co-worker at Abbott Labs invited me to be her guest at a private club in Waukegan. Before the evening was over, a young Navy chief petty officer introduced himself and asked me to dance. He was just one of many service men at the club that evening and I have to admit that I wasn't especially impressed. I returned to the club with my friend a few nights later and Chief John Blanchard was there again. He requested one more dance, and this time we talked a bit. When he asked me for a date, I accepted. Though it wasn't love at first sight, I do believe we began to fall in love on that first date.

While we were getting acquainted in the early days of our courtship, John kept bringing up the subject of my age and I kept avoiding the issue. I had always appeared older than my years. This had worked to my advantage in the past, and I didn't want it to fail me this time. I was afraid my 24-year-old Navy chief might break up with me if he knew I was only nineteen. He repeatedly assured me that age made absolutely no difference to him, yet he continued to ask. I finally responded, "How old do you think I am?" He replied that he thought I was closing in on 30, but it didn't matter that I was older. Older! I was overweight at that time, and the extra pounds must have made me look even older than usual. Much to my relief, when he found out I was younger, that didn't matter either. By this time Cupid's arrow had found its mark and we were hopelessly in love.

Even though the war was over, John's career in the Navy was not. He shipped out in December, 28 days after we met. He was assigned to six months sea duty aboard the USS Barnwell as it sailed from the West Coast to the East Coast. On parting, we promised to write each other every day — and we did. Our romance flourished and near Valentine's Day I received one of his letters, this time from the Canal Zone. In it, he asked me to marry him. I wrote back that night and eagerly accepted. By early March we were making plans for our June wedding and saving money for our honeymoon.

Whirlwind romances were common during the war and in the years that immediately followed. Back then, couples chose a song that would always have special meaning to them. This probably had to do with the uncertainty of the future, long deployments, and overseas duty. Music was something a couple could share even when separated by an ocean. Our song was "It Might As Well Be Spring." However, when I look back "Oh, What It Seemed to Be" kindles very special memories. Its lyrics tell the story of our whirlwind romance from meeting at a neighborhood dance, to our wedding in June, and the train ride we shared from Waukegan to Minneapolis on our honeymoon.

As John's return neared, I went to the best store in Waukegan to shop for a wedding outfit that would show off my new slim figure. This was an especially exciting day for me, because I hadn't told him that I had dieted and lost 40 pounds.

When I told the clerk that I wanted to buy a suit to wear for my wedding, she said, "I need to speak to the manager, but I'll be right back."

She returned after a few minutes and presented me with a pair of silk stockings. What a gift! I hadn't seen silk stockings for many years and hadn't dared to imagine wearing them on my wedding day. Of course, I searched until I found my wedding suit — a very nice one — at that store.

The day John came home, my brother Bill drove me to the Chicago station. Soon after the train rolled in, I spotted my tall petty officer working his way through the crowd. Of course, I was anxious to see John after six months but I must have felt a little shy. I didn't know how he would react to the new me, so I stood close to Bill for his brotherly support. John walked by twice without recognizing me! Then I couldn't wait any longer, I ran to him, and he took me in his arms. After our long-awaited greeting, he backed away, took a long survey of my new figure, and I could see that he was delighted with his "welcome home" surprise. John later explained why he'd walked past me. He had never met Bill and, standing together, we had looked like a couple. John assured me that had I been alone he would have found me right away.

John and I were married five days later at the Great Lakes Navy Chapel with Bill, Milt, Florence, Bobby, and my roommate-girlfriend witnessing our happy event. After the ceremony, Florence served a buffet for the small wedding party. Then John and I boarded a train headed for Squaw Point Resort on Sullivan Lake in Minnesota and our honeymoon. We had a wonderful time at the resort where we were referred to as "The Honeymoon Couple" and treated like royalty during our week's stay.

One of the happiest days of my life—the day I married Chief Petty Officer John Blanchard in June 1946. My attire included the suit I bought for this special day and silk stockings (a rare treasure during the war).

Blanchard Collection

Fishing was one of the main attractions of this resort. I didn't care to fish but I went out on the boat with John and enjoyed the time on the lake surrounded by beautiful scenery. One afternoon, the boat drifted into a patch of reeds close to shore. John asked me to hold his fishing pole while he and our guide maneuvered the boat back into deeper water. I sat with the pole in my hands, and to my surprise, a big bass took the bait. Although John helped me reel it in, we considered this fish my catch. The resort owner's wife prepared and served our fish to us for dinner that evening. It was delicious! I'm sure John would have enjoyed it more had he caught it himself. His only disappointment on the trip was that our one catch, all week, was mine.

After our honeymoon, we went to the farm so John could meet my parents. Mom wanted to make a good impression and worried about cooking for John. She asked me if I thought he would like pheasant. Northeastern Nebraska was known as pheasant country, and these birds were so plentiful that she canned some most years. I assured her that he would love them. So, my mother — a farmhouse gourmet — served a baked pheasant in her special cream sauce and John was very impressed.

After a few days with my family, we went back to Waukegan. John was still attached to the Great Lakes Naval Station but by August, he had orders to a new duty station: Charleston, South Carolina. I stayed in Waukegan until John found a little house to rent in North Charleston that came with an ice box and a pot belly stove. I could make the pot belly stove produce heat but my attempts to keep the ice box cold were a trial. The iceman came by every other day and I had trouble catching him. To this day, I swear the mule that pulled the ice wagon tiptoed past our place!

I couldn't find work in that area so we learned to live on John's salary, $181 a month plus a $37.50 housing allowance — if we hadn't been so *in love* we would have been miserable. John saved bus fare by catching a ride to the base when he could. I washed our clothes on a washboard in the bathtub and learned to cook something beyond the typical teenage fare of popcorn, Jell-O and fudge. After each payday I cooked a pot roast and served the leftovers in numerous ways until I used the last sliver. From there, the menu went downhill until payday and we could afford another pot roast.

Toward the end of our tour in South Carolina, John's father invited me to visit him in Tampa, Florida. He also invited John's mother, Naudine. John's parents had divorced several years earlier, and this was my first chance to meet either of them. I spent two weeks getting acquainted with my in-laws while John prepared for a change of duty station. After wrapping things up in South Carolina, he came to Florida for a brief visit with his parents and then we drove to Norfolk, Virginia. This would be my home while John went to sea aboard the USS Wyandot, a cargo ship headed for the Arctic carrying supplies for a Navy outpost there.

We bought an old car before John deployed, since new car production stopped during the war and had not resumed yet. I needed transportation but I had little driving experience, no mechanical knowledge, and knew nothing about car maintenance. One day, John helped me practice driving on a side street. We found a good spot to stop and he gave instructions while I changed a tire. A truck went by while John was standing with his hands on his hips watching me struggle with the tire. The driver stopped and backed up. We could see his lips moving and read the swear words as he pushed the door open. Hastily, we explained the situation. Once the trucker understood that John was a concerned husband — and not a big jerk — he closed his door and went on his way.

After settling me in Norfolk, John left and was out to sea for seven months while I learned the lonely side of being a Navy wife. I applied for work through an employment agency and they sent me to a trucking firm that needed a bookkeeper. After giving me a few days training, the boss's wife left me on my own. A day or so later, the boss called me into his private office, pulled a bottle of whiskey out of a drawer, and motioned to the couch. I knew what was on his mind. At only 20 years old, in a strange city, and with my husband out to sea — I was frightened beyond words. I reported this incident to the agency immediately, and the two people responded by laughing. They showed little concern. "Ol' Harry is up to his old tricks again," they said. Ol' Harry's behavior would likely bring a sexual harassment suit today — but back then, some men held the attitude that female employees were fair game. As it turned out, the agency came up with a job I liked better: bookkeeping machine operator at a wholesale food company. Before long, I made friends with a couple of other Navy wives. With friends and a better boss, I felt more secure but I was still lonely until John returned.

When John's ship arrived in Boston, he had orders to report to Great Lakes and I faced some new Navy wife responsibilities. I moved us out of the apartment in Norfolk, drove to D.C. to meet John, and we drove to our new duty station together. Great Lakes seemed like home and we could settle down for three years before John would come up for sea duty again.

I went back to work for Abbott Laboratories in Waukegan. They didn't have an opening for a bookkeeping machine operator so I worked in the accounts payable section. After waiting about a year for a bookkeeping machine operator opening, I began looking for work elsewhere. I took the Civil Service tests and applied for a position at Great Lakes Naval Station. When I was offered a position as a bookkeeping machine operator at the Great Lakes Naval Hospital, I took it. My career there lasted until I quit because of pregnancy—something women did universally in those days.

Once we arrived in Waukegan, we were close to Pender again and the Thanksgiving of 1948 was a family reunion: Vlasta, Milt, Bill, Earle, and I joined Mom and Dad for a delightful holiday. Since we would still be in Waukegan, we expected to enjoy a family celebration again the following year. Unfortunately, our plans changed when my brother was seriously injured during corn harvest that next fall.

Our family enjoyed Thanksgiving on the farm in 1948. Standing from the left; Bill, Helen, Earle, Vlasta, and Milt with Dad and Mom seated.

While Earle was oiling the moving roller on a corn-picking machine, his right sleeve caught in its powerful mechanism.

When he tried to free the sleeve with his left hand, both hands went into the rollers. Miraculously, he was able to remove his work boot and maneuver it into the rollers. The heavy boot jammed the machine, and Earle pulled his mangled hands free. Bleeding profusely, Earle managed to start another tractor that happened to be in the field and drove two and half miles to Pender. He passed out on the hospital steps. That Thanksgiving, he was in the hospital recovering from one of the many surgeries that would eventually give him some use of his hands, despite the loss of fingers. He was home a few weeks later, and all the siblings returned to the farm to be with him and our parents on Christmas.

I think we were all apprehensive as we made our travel plans. We didn't know how Earle was responding to his condition or how we would react upon seeing him. Our worries, however, were unfounded — Earle displayed an unbelievably positive attitude that put us all at ease. Even so, none of us could imagine that he would ever be able to support himself. That Christmas, Vlasta, Milt, Bill, and I made plans to make monthly contributions to Earl's support and gravely underestimated our younger brother's ability, courage, energy and ambition.

In a short time, Earle turned his knowledge of the livestock market into expertise and built a thriving business. Within a few years, he owned the largest livestock commission firm in Kansas City. Earle made us all proud — as a compassionate, caring person as well as a successful business man. Years later, after Earle's death, we learned that our brother was on call at the area hospitals: always available to offer encouragement and support to accident victims who had lost limbs.

Earle had a knack for making people feel comfortable in awkward situations. He was even able to empathize with the nervousness others felt about grasping a hand with no fingers. When offered a hand, he approached this friendly exchange with his ever-present positive attitude, kindness and a sense of humor. He always prepared the other person for his lack of grip. As he reached out, he explained that his handshake was like the new Oldsmobile with an automatic transmission: *No clutch!*

On our fourth anniversary, John and I decided that we wanted to start our family. John had another year at Great Lakes, and we hoped to enjoy an addition to our family before he was called upon for another tour of sea duty. As it turned out, John was by my side to welcome Bruce into our family in June 1951, the day after our fifth anniversary. We couldn't have been more proud! John beamed and my heart melted as I held our handsome newborn.

In a few days, we took our dear, sweet, little boy home. Then about two weeks later, the crying began. He screamed 12 hours a day, every day from noon to midnight. "Colic," the doctor said and assured us the crying would stop when the baby was three months old. "Just go home and enjoy him," he added. We tried but found no joy in dealing with a screaming infant. It was exhausting, stressful and difficult. As the daily crying continued, we tried every home remedy recommended to us. Nothing helped.

One afternoon, when Bruce was about a month old — and crying, of course — John called from the base. He said, "How would you like to go to Rio de Janeiro?" I hung up on him. With a screaming baby and a pile of diapers to fold, I was not receptive to this attempt at humor. In fact, I was livid! In the time it took to dial our number, the phone rang again, "Please stay on the line," he began. Then he told me that he had orders

Here I am, showing off our son, Bruce Blanchard, born in June 1951.

to Brazil, and the baby and I could go. With Bruce screaming in the background, I strained to hear every word as he told me that we would be leaving from New York in mid-December aboard the SS Argentina, a Moore McCormack Line cruise ship, and he was to report to language school in Washington D.C. almost immediately.

This left me in Waukegan, alone with a screaming baby, and a long list of tasks I had to do. I had to pack our baggage for the cruise and send it to New York where it would be in storage until the day we sailed. I had to get the furniture and house-hold items ready for the packers — deciding what would go to South America and what would stay in storage — Bruce and I both had to have shots, our car had to be sold in Waukegan (John would buy a new one in D.C. to ship to Rio), and I had to shop for American items we would need while we were in South America for the next two years.

One afternoon, while John was in D.C. attending language school and I was working on the "had to" list, I was suddenly aware that two-month-old Bruce had stopped crying. I ran to the crib fearing the worst but found my child sleeping peacefully. I couldn't believe it. When John called that evening I told him of the miracle. He told me that while walking after school that day, he found an open church and went in to pray. We compared notes and found that John's prayer time and Bruce's recovery happened about the same time. The next day, noon arrived—no crying, no colic! From that day forward I had a happy baby to enjoy.

I missed John, but the time went by fast. After I had taken care of all my tasks in Waukegan, Bruce and I went to the farm for a visit with my parents. Then, we boarded a train bound for New York City, the SS Argentina, and the fulfillment of the double-crown prophesy of my birth. It turned out, after all, the nurse had been right. That little Nebraska farm girl was about to take her first trip overseas.

In Rio, John would be assisting in training the Brazilians in the operation of two U.S. cruisers that had been sold to them early in the 1950s under the Mutual Defense Assistance Program. This was choice duty; it counted as sea duty, yet the family could come along. As an added benefit, the Brazilian government paid for our travel from New York to Rio de Janeiro and they provided first-class accommodations.

In mid-December, we boarded the SS Argentina and set sail on a two-and-a-half week voyage. All was well as we sailed down the East Coast until we came to rough waters off Cape Hatteras. As the ship began to sway with the swells, I discovered I was prone to sea sickness. During the next three days, John spent a lot of time wheeling six-month-old Bruce around the deck in a stroller. When I was able to join them, I could see that while I'd been confined to the cabin, John had been enjoying the cruise with his son. As soon as we stepped on deck, I heard, "Here comes John and the baby" and a group of very lovely Brazilian women rushed over to admire and coo over Bruce. The proud father — my devoted husband — relished this attention! Who could blame him?

All in all, it was a lovely cruise and we thoroughly enjoyed ourselves, although we found that first-class was really out of our class. Most of the first-class passengers were wealthy travelers whose evening attire included sable stoles and tuxedos. Some had celebrity status. A rumor made the rounds that the singer Carmen Miranda's relatives were aboard.

Once ashore, we lived in a furnished apartment in Ipanema until our furniture arrived. Then we moved to an apartment in another suburb, Leblon — our home for the next two years. Throughout our stay there, we had a full-time live-in maid. I soon realized that Rita was a godsend, because daily living in this South American country required a lot of effort that hadn't been required anywhere in my previous experience. Amoebic dysentery was common, as was tuberculosis, and all water we ingested had to be filtered and boiled, including water used for cooking. The few raw vegetables we could eat had to be soaked in a chlorinated solution and lack of refrigeration made it mandatory for meat to be sold the day it was killed. Thus, shopping for food from street vendors was a major task and a daily adventure. Despite all the inconveniences, we enjoyed the city and the people — forming a close circle of Brazilian and American friends.

We decided to have a second child while we were in Rio, and I had Rita's help with the household and childcare. My previous pregnancy and delivery had been difficult and this one proved to be troubled. Nonetheless, our beautiful daughter, Cheryl, arrived safely in November 1952, and we were delighted to add this baby girl to our family. Born in Brazil to United States nationals, she was considered a citizen of both countries until she reached 21, at which time she chose U.S. citizenship.

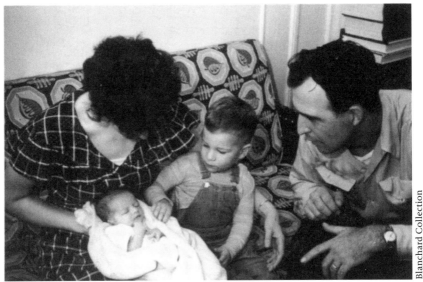

While we were living in Rio in November of 1952, John, Bruce, and I welcomed Cheryl into our family.

Our time in Rio was the highlight of my Navy wife years. Having Rita's help relieved much of the pressure of being a mom to two little ones, and I enjoyed my time spent with the children as well as our life there. Later, we returned to the States for an assignment in Washington D.C. where we lived in a two story townhouse with a basement. The frequent trips up and down stairs used muscles I didn't remember I had, and chasing two toddlers full-time was a new experience for me. I became so exhausted that I went to the doctor thinking I had some terminal disease. As it turned out, I was just suffering from *motherhood with no Rita*. Fortunately, I was young and strong — and with more time to get used to my new situation, I recovered completely.

John's next assignment was sea duty aboard the USS Lake Champlain—home base: Mayport, Florida. We rented a nice house with a big yard in Jacksonville where the kids and I lived while John's ship was at sea. He was away in the Mediterranean because of a Middle East crisis. It was my first time alone with the children and—oh, how we missed John! He wrote often but, of course, the children couldn't read. We didn't think they could relate to their father's words spoken with my voice. So, John recorded himself reading the children's favorite

Bruce and Cheryl listening to Daddy's voice reading one of their favorite books that he'd prerecorded before he left for an assignment, January 1956.

story books before he left and, through the miracle of modern technology available in the 1950s, Bruce and Cheryl heard their father's voice almost every day that he was away.

These days, I live in San Diego with a view of San Diego Bay. And when I see Navy ships coming back to port, I think of the joy the children and I shared when the Lake Champlain came in and we saw John on deck.

In September 1956, John received orders to report to the Naval Training Center in San Diego as an instructor in the Interior Communications School. This was to be his last duty before retirement from the Navy and the end of my years as Navy wife.

Chapter 5

Back to Work

We arrived in San Diego, and a new chapter of my life began to unfold. For the first time since we married, John and I could live our life without thinking about a move to the next duty station. We could settle permanently in one place. We could think about buying a house and perhaps getting a dog.

We bought a house in Allied Gardens, a new development at the edge of San Diego, north of Interstate 8, located on a canyon rim above Mission Valley. It was 1956 and dairy cattle roamed the grassy meadows along the San Diego River, which wound its way through the valley between towering canyon walls. Today Mission Valley is home to two major shopping centers, the Charger's Stadium and a mass of condominium complexes in the heart of Metropolitan San Diego.

We arrived in San Diego in October and stayed with Navy friends until our new house was ready. By November, we were settling into our new home — unpacking and meeting most of our neighbors. Then we began our landscaping project: a Southern California classic of foundation shrubs, shade trees and a lawn that stayed green all year.

Bruce entered kindergarten with Cheryl following the next fall — and I began to experience schools in a new way. I volunteered for Parent-Teacher Association (PTA) at my children's school and participated in many of my kids' activities. They joined Cub Scouts and Brownies, while I took great pleasure in my budding role as a typical suburban wife and mother.

Bruce, Cheryl and I pose for a photo before going to an after-school event. As a typical suburban mom, I joined PTA, and did my part in Cub Scouts, and Brownies.

Before long we decided to add a dog to our family. We chose a large pup with a smooth coat and floppy ears, a Weimaraner-Labrador mix. Clancy — who, despite her name was a female — won our hearts and earned a reputation as the *neighborhood* dog. She may have been best known for her habit of eating honeybees she snatched out of the air. We thought letting Clancy have pups would be a good educational experience for Bruce and Cheryl. John ran advertisements twice in the local newspaper's pet section, promising pick of the litter to the owner of a mate for Clancy. When that failed, my husband's sense of humor took control and he ran an ad in the personals — you can imagine the responses to that! We were finally contacted by a lady who wanted her Weimaraner to, as she put it, "have some fun." A few weeks after this *one night stand,* it became apparent that Clancy was in the family way. As the due date neared, John prepared a whelping box in the garage. When the big day came, John narrated while Clancy labored to produce her twelve puppies. Early in the process, he turned his back to Clancy. As he explained that a doctor would help a woman giving birth by doing some of the things that Clancy was doing; he was completely unaware that Clancy was tending her firstborn and instinctively polishing off the placenta. John was surprised to see a look of sheer horror on Bruce's face.

Our son bolted from the scene shouting, "I never want to be a doctor!"

Once Cheryl was in first grade and in school all day, I began to feel restless. The yard was landscaped and designed for "low-maintenance." We had permanent-press clothing and a houseful of modern appliances. After the household chores were done, I had several hours of spare time each day. I needed to keep busy but I could only clean so many closets and endure so many neighborhood coffee-and-gossip sessions before boredom set in. One morning, while cleaning out some old files, I found my Civil Service records. I think what happened that day can best be described as serendipity. Although I didn't have any intention of returning to work in the near future, I was curious. Was I still in the system — and employable by the government — or would I have to take a battery of tests before applying for a new position? With time on my hands and nothing better to do that morning, I decided to call and find out.

The gentleman in the personnel office told me that I was, indeed, in the system and that the Navy Electronics Laboratory (NEL, later referred to as "the Center") had an opening for a bookkeeping machine operator. He said this position had been open for quite some time and he had been unable to send a qualified person to the Lab to apply. He asked if I would go talk to them as a favor. My afternoon was free that day, and Point Loma was a lovely place to visit. So, I decided to get out of the house and take a drive to NEL — just to talk to them. I liked the place. What's more, they liked me and made an offer. I wanted the job.

After my visit to NEL that afternoon, John and I discussed my job offer at length. I was excited and I saw this as an opportunity to enrich my life. The more we talked about it, the more I wanted to accept the job. My husband, however, being a pretty smart guy, wasn't pleased at all. Coming home to a good meal, well-tended children, an immaculate house and a manicured yard would be hard to give up. I didn't blame him, and I promised that I would not ask him for help with the household. We finally came to an agreement with the "no help" stipulation guaranteed.

In the two weeks between my acceptance and actually going to work, neighbors and friends almost went into panic mode.

The coffee clutch gals were appalled that I would even think of going to work. It just wasn't done in our neighborhood, they said — men supported their families and women stayed home with their children. A male friend of ours took me aside for a "heart to heart." Ignoring the fact that operating a bookkeeping machine was considered women's work, he scolded me for taking a job a man could be doing and thus snatching food from the mouths of babes. Another friend of John's said that by going to work, I made it look like John was not able to provide for his family. He said John would be shamed in front of his male friends.

I never did receive encouragement from family or friends. Still, I knew what my decision had to be. Operating a bookkeeping machine may not sound very exciting, but I enjoyed it, and I wanted to do it. I was bored and going back to work was something I felt I had to do for myself.

At that time, two thirds of working women were employed in clerical, service and sales positions. Bookkeeping, a clerical duty, was on the right side of the gender gap. So-called "women's work," however, had always extended into the professions: nursing and teaching.

Of course, history has recorded a few exceptions in most professions. By the late 1950s, a growing number of women were earning professional degrees, becoming physicians, dentists, lawyers and politicians. We had women occupying seats in the U.S. House and Senate. In fact, Senator Margaret Chase Smith, a Republican from Maine, ran in several Republican presidential primaries in 1964 and became the first woman to have her name placed in nomination for the presidency at the national convention of a major political party. When the roll was called that year, Senator Smith came in second to Barry Goldwater.

As women gained political clout, advances in equal rights and opportunities came slowly. After an eighteen year effort, John F. Kennedy signed an equal pay bill into law in 1963. At that time, the wage gap was 59%: women earned 59 cents for every dollar men earned. By 2006, women had moved ahead but still lagged behind with a 77% wage gap.

As I prepared to go back to work, leaving the kids in someone else's care was a great concern. I did not want them to feel neglected or disadvantaged because their mother worked. At first, they went to a trusted neighbor's house after school and stayed in her care until we arrived home from work. During that hour, they enjoyed a snack and played with the neighborhood kids just as they did when I was home. Later we hired a sitter until we felt Bruce and Cheryl were mature enough to stay home on their own. I never saw any evidence that my working damaged the kids in any way.

One afternoon when I arrived home early, Bruce made a point of hugging me and telling me that he missed me. Then he dashed out to play. His brief adoring display lost its flavor when he stayed out past dinnertime, and I had to comb the neighborhood and bring him home. As an adult, Cheryl said that the main thing she remembered about me going to work was that she earned big money—a whopping $5 per week—for doing chores. She also said that she enjoyed the freedom she had as a so-called "latchkey kid."

I kept my promise and didn't ask John for help around the house. We bought a dryer and I cut back on closet cleaning. I organized my housework with a tight weekend schedule. Saturday, I cleaned house and did the laundry. I cooked on

Sunday afternoon and froze meals for the coming week. The kids helped out. They happily agreed to take on more responsibility with an increase in their weekly allowance — bribery is a wonderful tool.

I enjoyed every aspect of working outside the home. I worked with a good group in the accounting department and made some lasting friendships. I was one of three operators and I still keep in touch with one of the others. I carpooled with three coworkers from our housing tract, Allied Gardens. Two worked in the technical area and I enjoyed some very interesting conversations during our commute. I actually looked forward to the drive to and from work on Highway 8. At that time, it was a pastoral two lanes with a stop light at Texas Street. Now, traveling Interstate 8 through Mission Valley is a rush-hour nightmare with 8 lanes of bumper-to-bumper, stop-and-go traffic, and Texas Street is a freeway interchange.

Before long, John adjusted to having a working wife and decided to help, mostly with the yard but he always did the floors and the bathrooms. Although our household was running smoothly, we knew we would have a childcare problem when the school year ended. We had been comfortable leaving the children in someone else's care an hour after school but leaving them every day, all day, for three months was a concern. That spring, John and I crunched the numbers and found that the additional expense of hiring a reliable sitter, full-time, for the summer meant that I couldn't afford to work. So, I resigned my job to stay home with the children.

About a year and a half later, in January 1961, I received a call from the personnel department at the Center asking if I would consider a six month temporary job in a scientific department. Thinking this might work out — the San Diego school year ends in mid-June—I went for the interview. Although every-one knew that almost every aspect of this job would be new to me, they offered me the position and I accepted.

The Center was bringing in the newest technology and moving into the computer age with a CDC 1640 from the Control Data Corporation. It's easy to smirk at all that machinery now; the home computer I have on my desk these days will do much more, much faster, than the entire roomful of then state-of-the-art technology acquired by the Center in 1961. But at the time, it truly was cutting-edge equipment. I wasn't allowed near the massive unit except for a peek into the area where it did its magic with for-mulas, equations and numbers. I saw a massive collection of electronic components with blinking lights and whir-ring motors that filled a temperature-controlled, air-filtered room. Programmers talked to the machine using IBM punch cards. The computer language was FORTRAN or the Center's unique language, NELIAC.

I didn't do any programming, but I worked closely with those who did and used information generated by the com-puter. Obviously, this position required a lot of on-the-job training and would have been a new experience for just about anyone. I was the lucky choice, and this introduction to the computer in its infancy opened the door to my future.

My new position was in the Signal Physics Division. The Department of Defense description of my job sounded very impressive and a little frightening. I was to participate in a study, requested by the Advanced Research Projects Agency in Washington D.C., concerning the feasibility of hydro-acoustic detection of nuclear explosions detonated in violation of a pos-sible nuclear test moratorium. My duties were to give sub-pro-fessional assistance to the scientific group who were currently engaged in making this study. Simply put, I researched data that was used by this scientific group and performed a variety of other tasks including keypunch work, setting up filing systems and typing.

Most of my time, however, was dedicated to drafting scientific graphs, schematics and charts. Working long hours at a light table, I translated data from computer printouts into graphics to prepare pen and ink drawings that supplemented the final reports issued by the group. Sometimes I spent days working on one graph. As I neared the end, I held my breath and prayed that the ink would not smear and the pen would not release an extra dot of ink. Some of the intricate graphs I drew were two feet wide and six feel long. This was my first exposure to this type of precision work and I absolutely loved it.

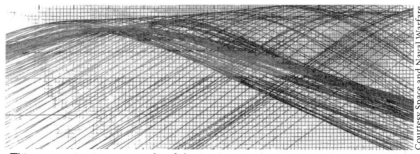

This ray tracing is an example of the intricate and tedious graphics work I did while working in the Signal Physics Division.

Courtesy Space and Naval Warfare Systems San Diego

At the end of my six-month assignment, the division head asked if I would remain in my position and become a permanent employee. I loved the work and this was a tempting offer but I had promised John and the kids that I would only work until school was out for the summer. So, I declined the offer.

He replied, "The position will be available for you in the fall."

Unfortunately, the Center came under a hiring freeze a short time later. John and I were both disappointed. We were looking forward to the extra income. By this time, he had retired from the Navy and enrolled in college. With his change in schedule and the children growing older, childcare had become less of an issue.

That fall, we decided that I could finally go to work full-time. When the job at the Center fell through, I applied for a position in the San Diego City Schools Administration Office. School districts often take some time processing applications, so I settled in for the wait.

Meanwhile, in January 1962, someone from the Center personnel office called to ask if I would be interested in a supervisory position (GS-5) in the Technical Information Division. Of course, I was. "General Schedule" (GS) is the name used to describe a pay scale used by the majority of white collar personnel — professional, technical, administrative and clerical — in the civil service of the Federal government of the United States. So, an offer of a GS-5 position would be a good one.

We met for an interview and I was hired. About a month later, the school district called to request an interview with me. They were too late. I sometimes wonder what would have happened had that call come first. As it turned out, my full-time position in the Technical Information Division launched a career at the Center that would bring me into Toastmasters a few years later and see me through to retirement.

As head of distribution, I supervised three clerks. According to the job description, our small group was responsible for the cold-type composition and distribution of all formal publications and technical reports issued by the Center. We compiled distribution lists in each field of research, determined print order, and readied all publications and reports for mailing.

In reality, our four-woman group processed the material generated by the scientists at the Center who were prolific writers sharing their scientific findings in written reports. We were responsible for turning their rough drafts into pages ready to send to the printer. Two of my clerks did the "cold-type composition" which was much more difficult than typing letters and memos. The text of these reports was peppered with formulas and equations and there was no room for error. The other clerk was my assistant. The Center published hundreds of reports, and after they were printed — usually in batches in excess of a hundred — we prepared them for mailing and addressed them to the recipients on each document's unique distribution list.

A great deal of time was required for typing those lists and addressing the envelopes using the old addressograph-type machine. Since I had been introduced to the computer in my previous job, I envisioned using such technology to save time generating the list and addressing the envelopes. I devised a method using IBM punch cards and a tabulating machine that resided in the computer area. My idea proved successful and extremely time saving. The Center gave me a special award for this achievement, and I wrote a paper which was sent to all the other Navy laboratories for implementation.

That spring, the hiring freeze was lifted, and I received a call from the head of the Signal Physics Division asking if I wanted to transfer back to that department on a permanent assignment. I wanted to. However, I was involved in a large project in distribution and felt I couldn't leave my current position after such a short time on the job.

My mother played a part in this decision — I remembered her telling me, "Finish the work you have obligated yourself to do." A year seemed sufficient to fulfill this commitment, so in January of 1963, I finally transferred back to the Signal Physics Division and the job I enjoyed so much.

I returned to my old boss, Tom McMillian, with a new title, *physical science technician*. Although this may sound impressive, it was actually a downgrade from GS-5 to GS-4, but I took the downgrade gladly because it put me in a spot with potential for further advancement.

In this position, I worked on two reports. The first was the analysis of records of low-frequency acoustic waves in the air produced by nuclear tests titled "Hardtack." I prepared all the artwork (83 figures) in camera-ready copy and wrote a small portion of the text—receiving credit as one of three authors of this then secret document.

I also co-authored a second report that analyzed the underwater signals from a series of large explosions. For this project, called "Operation Sailor Hat," I used magnetic tapes from fixed land monitoring stations to determine the time of a sound signal's arrival, its amplitude, speed, and sources of probable reflections. Preparing for these studies required that I take some college courses.

While attending college, I also needed to study outside class, continue working full-time, and tend to my duties at home. For the first time in my life, I felt overwhelmed. As with all things, this eventually passed. After I completed the needed studies, my routine returned to normal. I stayed in this position for over two years before qualifying for a GS-5 physical science technician.

Then, as was prone to happen, the Center reorganized and several departments shifted locations. The head of the Signal Physics Division was given management of the Fleet Operational Readiness Check Site (FORACS) program. And so, Tom McMillian, my boss, was named to head that program. When he moved, he took some of us with him.

Chapter 6

FORACS

Venturing into Man's Territory

When I made the move to FORACS, I didn't know what to expect. This was a new program created by the Navy to solve a specific problem, and there were no formal job descriptions.

The FORACS program had been developed by The Applied Physics Lab (APL) at the University of Washington to solve a problem the Navy was experiencing with its sonar and weapons systems. In tests and war games, the new technically-advanced torpedoes were missing their targets. This imprecision rendered these weapons useless, and the Navy needed to know whether the problem was with the shipboard sensors that provided information to the torpedoes' guidance systems or with the design of the torpedoes themselves. Initial tests determined that the problem was with the accuracy of the shipboard sensors and FORACS was developed to test these sensors. The people brought into the program had a task to do and that was to follow the test procedures created by APL: gather the data generated at the test site, analyze that information, and write reports that would provide the Navy with a measure of the ships' combat readiness.

At the time, the United States found itself embroiled in the Cold War with the Soviet Union. Our work to perfect these weapons was considered an important part of the U.S. government's effort to protect Americans from this compelling threat.

During the weeks of transition, I completed my tasks at the Signal Physics Division spending a few more hours in the FO-RACS office each week. While I was dividing my time between the two departments, Tom McMillian recommended me for a promotion from GS-5 to GS-7, the advancement progression for the physical technician series. While this was being considered, I went through a desk audit. For a full day, an auditor followed me from one department to the other, observing my work, asking questions, and taking copious notes. Tom was surprised that a promotion at this level would require so much investigation and we were both pleased when I eventually received it.

At that time, the first two ranges — sensor test sites — were in operation: FORACS I at San Clemente Island about 70 miles off the coast of Southern California and FORACS II at Guantanamo, Cuba. These ranges were operated by contract personnel — mostly engineers and technicians from large companies such as Philco-Ford and RCA — and each contractor had his own established methods of handling the data. When our office at the Center began receiving reports written by the contract personnel at these two range sites, we found that their methods of reporting the data were incompatible. As a result, analyzing the data and compiling it into summary reports to send Washington was difficult, if not impossible.

During the Cold War, such a setback was unacceptable. My first assignment with FORACS was to review the reports from each site and compile letters containing comments, corrections, and suggestions for improvement that would make these data reports more uniform. At first, my supervisor carefully reviewed each letter before he attached his signature and sent it to the range manager who had filed the report. In a short while, however, my ability to critique the reports proved itself, and he authorized me to sign and send the letters myself.

Blanchard Collection

In 1971, my first FORACS assignment was to find a way to improve the uniformity of the data reports from the FORACS ranges.

As it turned out, acquiring the uniform data needed for compiling the summary reports required more than a few letters. We needed to create formal guidelines for a consistent method of handling data to be used at all the ranges. In time, we decided that a computer program that would merge the data from the ranges was needed along with a data bank to store the results of the range tests for later analysis. After the program was written by a computer specialist, I took the responsibility for putting the data bank into operation. Suddenly, my job expanded from writing critique letters to training the range engineers. This meant that I would travel to the ranges where, basically, I would tell well-educated men how to do their job in areas where—in those days—the only women were secretaries and computer operators. To say I was uncomfortable with this new situation is an understatement. I had graduated from normal school for grade school teachers, not college. My education qualified me to teach the first eight grades in a one-room school house. Who was I to train college graduates with engineering degrees?

I could see that I was headed down a rocky path leading to rough waters. The rocky path meandered through my own neighborhood of Allied Gardens, and 1966 proved to be a tough year in my personal life. John's position with the Naval Undersea Center—a sister Center located bayside in Point Loma—seldom took him away from home. That year, however, he spent six months (February through July) aboard a research ship in the Bering Sea.

While I was facing new challenges at work and shouldering full responsibility at home, my life suddenly took a misstep along that rocky path. John's mother, Naudine, underwent surgery. When her doctor came out of the operating room, he told me that he had removed a malignant tumor, and we should think about calling John home. I decided to delay the call until the lab report confirmed the diagnosis. All weekend—alone—I struggled with this disturbing news. When the lab report finally came, I was relieved to learn that the tumor was benign, and Naudine was on her way to recovery. She would require my help, which I was happy to give, of course!

About this same time, I was diagnosed with an ulcer. In those days, they treated an ulcer by cutting the vagus nerve, and I was scheduled for surgery as soon as John returned. Fortunately, Bruce and Cheryl were in their teens, and I was very pleased to find them responsible and helpful during these difficult months.

The benefits for Civil Service employees include vacation time and sick leave so the time-off I needed was available. Progress, however, did not stand still. Soon after I returned to work, I received my first travel orders and John strongly disapproved. I think the hardest part for him came from his Navy days — the idea that a woman would be in a Navy facility, training men, was not acceptable. The first trip was the most difficult. I will never forget his reaction when I told him I had to make a trip to San Clemente Island. Speaking in very clear terms, he questioned my boss's intelligence in sending a woman to the test site. This was followed by, "Who do you think you are to be telling engineers how to handle data?" He was only a little chauvinistic.

I was already nervous about the assignment and I had these same thoughts bouncing around in my head. At that moment, I wondered if I had just seen an example of the attitude I could expect from the engineers. This was new territory for me and I would have welcomed some encouragement at home. When it didn't come, I shed some tears and prayed for courage.

Once more, I could hear my mother say, "You have committed to do a job; do your best." I was determined to do just that.

By the time I made that first trip to the range on San Clemente Island, more ranges were in the process of being added. Personnel from FORACS III in Hawaii came to the Center for training, and I was assigned to take a female computer technician to San Clemente to observe a test during the day and watch the computer operators work the data that night. At that time, the Navy facility on San Clemente Island was *all male* and the quarters for men included barracks and a few guest cottages. When my boss requested accommodations for two women he was told that this was impossible. He persisted and was informed that two guards would be placed outside the guest cottage where we stayed, and our project would be billed for their services. It was then decided that we ladies would fly out for the day-time tests and return to shore that evening without observing the data processors that night. According to this altered plan, the computer operator and I observed the tests on San Clemente Island and then went to Anaheim where we watched the analysis procedure the next day. I really enjoyed this experience and I saw that I had a valuable opportunity and accepted the challenge of developing it into a full-time meaningful position for myself.

Early in 1967, our family experienced a duel crisis. Dad came to visit and suffered a stroke while he was in San Diego. About that same time, John had his first heart attack. To make it a little easier on me, the doctors put them in the same hospital where they both received excellent care and soon recovered.

However, this was an eye-opening, attitude-adjusting experience for us. Prior to his heart attack, we considered John a healthy young man with many productive years ahead. He had cashed in his military life insurance, and we used the money for home improvements including a large family room, covered patio and swimming pool — John loved to entertain. The plan was that he would buy a new life insurance policy later. After the heart attack, of course, this was not possible. John was now very pleased that I was working and had a decent job. So was I. We were even more pleased when I was promoted from GS-7 to GS-9 that year.

As far as I knew at the time, this promotion went through without a problem. I was later told, however, that there were questions about the promotion and two people above me in our department met with personnel. They confirmed the accuracy of the description of my job and performance in the written request for the promotion. I think the questions arose because a woman without a college degree doing work I did with the FORACS ranges, and the fact that I was the lead author for a technical report entitled "FORACS Analysis Data Reduction and Analysis for the AN/3Q3-18-46 Buoy Test Results" was unusual.

My next travel assignment was to Hawaii to discuss data analysis and report writing at FORACS III in Hawaii. On this trip, I stayed at the apartment of the computer operator I had accompanied to San Clemente. She lived near Diamond Head. Except for this familiar landmark, I was completely unfamiliar with the lush-green tropical island and her neighborhood. That night my heart pounded as I was suddenly awakened by blood-curdling sounds: lions roaring and elephants trumpeting! She hadn't thought to tell me that she lived near the zoo, and these were the ordinary sounds of the night.

After I returned from this trip, my supervisor decided I should learn something about the fleet sonar systems and arranged for me to attend a two-week course called "Sonar Familiarization" at the Anti-submarine Warfare School in San Diego. As I expected, these young Navy men were puzzled when they arrived in the classroom and found a civilian woman in their midst. The instructor explained my need for the class, they seemed to accept the situation, and I settled in as just another student.

Most of the FORACS sites are located where year-round tem-
peratures are mild. At that time, however, one was located in
Massachusetts. My third trip was to FORACS IV, located on
the very tip of Cape Cod near Provincetown. In November of
1967, New England weather was bad, with the area suffering
record snowfall.

The group from the Center who were traveling to the site from
the Center included engineers and computer operators, there to
train their counterparts, plus my boss's secretary and me. The
site was newly established with a trailer that temporarily housed
the computer equipment and an apartment that served as the
office and quarters for the male members of our group.

Cape Cod, like most East Coast summer spots is almost
abandoned in winter. By the time we arrived, all the summer
tourists were gone and all the businesses except for one grocery store and the Provincetown Inn were closed.

The engineers from the Center bunked in the apartment
while the secretary and I found reasonably-priced rooms to
rent from one of the locals, Tillie, who lived a short distance
away. Tillie's spare bedrooms were Spartan: linoleum floors,
a pull-chain light in the middle of the ceiling, a shared bath-
room, and no kitchen privileges. The restaurant at the inn was
expensive, so the secretary and I cooked and ate at the apart-
ment/office with the men.

I was away from home for two weeks on this trip, and of
course I wanted to keep in touch with John. I called a couple of
times from the office but couldn't really talk with everyone in
the room. When I got home John told me had called the board-
ing house and when he asked for me, Tillie said to him, "Oh,
them girls. Don't know where they are. They come in all hours
of the night." Fortunately, John understood that we worked

long hours when we had ships on the range and he wasn't surprised that I was out late. I was always so thankful that we had complete trust in one another, whoever was on travel.

FORACS IV was headed by an engineer who had transferred from the shipyard in Boston and I was there to train him in FORACS analysis and report writing. I sensed right away that he was uncomfortable with me, always polite but cool. He was warmer and more at ease with the secretary. However, he was in a new position, learning new tasks, and it is possible that only part of his apparent discomfort came from having a female instructor.

With three ships scheduled for the range that week, we worked long hours while he was under pressure to learn our requirements for collecting and processing the data. At least one night we worked until 1:00 AM and we hit a few snags that delayed things.

In preparing the report on each ship, we first received the data from the tests in computer listings. Then, we reviewed the data output to catch any possible errors in data input. Next, we determined the coordinates of the graphs to be printed. After that, we compared the results against the standards set for that particular system and wrote the analysis that would accompany the graph. Finally, we organized and formatted all the material for printing the report that would be sent to our office at the Center.

One night as we reviewed the data, I pointed out that the gyrocompass results were unusual and asked for a review of the data and a new computer output. When this was done I still believed an error existed, in fact, I was sure. I told them that I could not put this result in the report. The range manager and engineers from the Center were shaking their heads — and I could pretty well read their minds — as they went over the data again. I convinced them to try a third time, and they found that there had indeed been a mistake in the readings, and the data were incorrect. Once the correction was made, we finished the report. This incident gave my credibility a boost and helped improve the attitudes of the FORACS IV personnel as well as the training team from the Center.

The following May, I received a Sustained Superior Performance Award from the Center for meeting many "unique problems" during that visit to FORACS IV. My citation stated that during those initial tests at the FORACS IV range my "advice on data analysis and report writing training was invaluable to the new personnel there" and that I was "often called upon to provide assistance to the Fleet Engineering Support Division on topics related to FORACS data." Of course, receiving this award helped prove my worth in many ways, including the quality of training I had provided at the site. A month later — June, 1968 — I was promoted to GS-11.

Until I made the journey to Cape Cod, my travel had typically involved only a few nights away from home. This two-week trip, however, left John and the kids on their own much longer than they had experienced before. I had confidence that John could manage well in my absence. However, a few days after I returned home, I fixed pancakes for breakfast and learned the truth. When I gave the kids their plates, I was surprised to see them turn their pancakes over before they added butter and syrup. "Why did you do that?" I asked.

They both replied, "Because Dad puts the burnt on the bottom."

This was one incident that led me to believe things were a little different when I was away. It assured me that I was missed at home just as much as I missed them when I was away. I never requested travel but I went when I was asked to go. It was difficult in the early years when the kids were young. Nevertheless, they grew up — as all kids do — graduated high school and eventually moved out to build their own lives.

By Christmas 1968, Bruce and Cheryl were quite mature and capable of helping John manage the home front when I was on travel. (From the left - Bruce, Cheryl, Helen, and John.)

Blanchard Collection

A few years later, John passed away, and I found myself alone. My job at the Center, and Toastmasters, helped fill the void, gave me a reason to face each new day, and provided travel opportunities I would not have enjoyed otherwise.

As it turned out, the double-crown prophecy of my birth was to be fulfilled many times throughout my career and after retirement. Travel associated with my positions at the Center and my Toastmasters experience took me overseas, and I chalked up hundreds of thousands of miles. I traveled to FORACS ranges in Honolulu, Hawaii (11 times), Guantanamo, Cuba,

St. Croix in the Virgin Islands, and the Atlantic Undersea Test and Evaluation Center (AUTEC) range in the Bahamas.

Later, when NATO became interested in FORACS, I traveled to Stavanger, Norway. During this time, I became very comfortable traveling alone, and after I retired, I toured Europe for pleasure on my own. Much of my confidence was acquired in the FORACS years in those places that were not designed to accommodate females.

In August of 1969, I made a short visit to the AUTEC range on Andros Island in the Bahamas. AUTEC had requested assistance from my team in training their personnel to conduct FORACS tests. This would be the first of nine trips I would make to Andros Island. When my friends heard that I was going to the Bahamas, they all envied me. Andros Island however, is not the typical tropical paradise they envisioned. It is still the least developed island in the chain.

The people who worked at the site lived an austere life, to say the least. They were quartered in barracks and ate in a mess hall. Fishing and boating were about the only pleasurable activities available. I spent two days there and then flew to our range at Guantanamo, Cuba.

Guantanamo is a U.S. Navy Base located in Cuba, a Communist country. Since Fidel Castro cut off the fresh water supply to the base in 1964, Guantanamo has been completely self sufficient with its own power and water. The Navy made this possible by relocating a desalination water processing plant from Point Loma, California, to Guantanamo. And so it was that I could find one familiar sight in this very unfamiliar land.

Upon my arrival at Guantanamo, I expected to follow our plan, which was for me to stay with a female employee who lived on base. But the flight arrived late and the driver who met the plane took me to the Bachelor Officers Quarters (BOQ) at the base. He told me to stay there the rest of the night and he would take me to the range the next morning. After being shown to my room, I set my wake-up alarm and tried to grab a few hours sleep. Rustling noises kept me awake, and upon investigation, I found lizards crawling on the window screen — it seemed they wanted in! My most startling discovery, however, was yet to come.

The next morning as I made my way toward the front of the building to meet my ride, I met a man apparently returning from a shower. He was completely nude and was swinging a towel around instead of using it for cover. Upon seeing me, his eyes widened and, in perhaps the swiftest Navy maneuver ever, he flipped the towel around his waist. Certain now that I'd invaded *man's territory*, I didn't slow down — I kept walking, eyes on the door. While I waited for my ride I heard a loud and very salty outburst directed toward the young sailor at the registration desk.

Later while I was being introduced to the military personnel on base, one officer turned red-faced; I'm sure I did, too. I smile when I think of the incident now. But back then, it was extremely embarrassing. I was nearing the time when I would seek help from Toastmasters in becoming more comfortable making training presentations. Though I don't think all my years of Toastmaster's experience could have prepared me for this Navy encounter.

Chapter 7

Toastmasters — Career Booster

By 1970, I had made several presentations. I was secure in my knowledge of the subject and the accuracy of the material I presented. Yet entering a roomful of men with engineering degrees was still intimidating. I had never grown comfortable standing before these professionals. Butterflies and shaking knees were my constant companions, and I just could not overcome my fear.

I still had little support at home. After discovering his heart condition, John had to deal with mixed emotions. He knew that, in reality, I needed a good job to assure my financial security. Still, he didn't like the travel and he harbored some of those Navy-days chauvinistic thoughts: a woman should not be doing that job. His attitude left me in turmoil and kept me wondering how many FORACS engineers shared his feelings.

Another challenge trailed me almost everywhere I traveled. I was often the lone woman in men's territory — military outposts — and special arrangements had to be made for my privacy and safety. I tried to fortify myself by remembering that my boss entrusted me to provide essential information to these men. The reports they sent to us had to be consistent, based on data collected and analyzed in a like manner on all the FORACS ranges. Otherwise, all their efforts would have no lasting value to the Navy. Knowing this, and gaining experience, I still lacked the necessary confidence.

When I picked up that copy of the Center's newsletter, the *Calendar*, I thought I had found the answer. I needed to learn to "present with confidence" as the Toastmasters advertisement promised. Of course, I was disappointed to learn that Toastmasters was for men only, and although they offered Toastmistress meetings for women, there wasn't one at the Center. Worse yet, when I tried to launch one I couldn't find any other women interested in joining.

Again, I was fortunate. A past district governor with years of Toastmasters experience, Bob Bolam, understood that career women needed the organization as much as men. Looking back, I believe he had exceptional foresight and could see the time coming when women would need Toastmasters training on equal footing with men. And by the same token, those "men on the move" would need to have experience speaking to professional women.

He appealed to the membership on my behalf, and I was allowed to join the Center's Toastmasters club on June 18, 1970. I was made to feel welcome, and the entire club fully supported my membership. When Toastmasters World Headquarters insisted on a name to replace the initial on my membership application, the Center's club members helped solve my gender problem. They used Table Topics to choose the best replacement for the "H" and one speaker argued convincingly for "Homer." So, *Helen* became *Homer*. None of us could imagine then, that Homer would become a part of Toastmasters history, and roughly 30 years later, some sessions offered at Toastmasters conferences would be located in the Homer Room.

I began to benefit from my Toastmasters experience almost immediately. While learning the ropes of public speaking, I discovered that the Toastmasters organization is geared to help speakers who feel intimidated by their audiences for various reasons — it was good to know I shared a common problem. Building confidence through practice in a safe environment is the key to conquering the fear of public speaking.

I discovered increased confidence early in my Toastmasters experience. I had attended only a few meetings when my FORACS boss arranged for me to attend a week-long management training course in San Francisco. Of the twenty-four people attending the course, four of us were women — a five to one ratio. I could sense the nervousness of the three other women. Their hesitant speech patterns and body language gave them away as they briefly introduced themselves to the mostly-male audience. I knew I would have performed at the same poor level had it not been for Toastmasters. For, although I had not been a member very long, I was able to stand and deliver my introduction with ease. That experience sold me on Toastmasters completely. I could see the potential for gaining leadership training — as well as communication skills — and I wanted it all.

Once I realized the true value of the organization, I let it be known that I wanted to do my part. Toastmaster Clubs elect officers every six months and there is a natural progression in which one can be elected to higher office. The normal order for our club at that time was sergeant at arms, treasurer, secretary, administrative vice president, vice president education and club president. Sometime later, a vice president membership and vice president public relations replaced the administrative vice president. This exact order isn't followed in all clubs but it was in ours at the time. Once a person accepted the nomination and was elected to a beginning office — with their consent — that person could follow the progression and be voted into the next office.

So, when January of 1971 rolled around, I was willing to take the responsibility for one of the beginning offices, I accepted the nomination and was elected treasurer. The sergeant at arms prepared the meeting room and, at that time, this first position was held by a member who had an office nearby with a convenient place to keep the supplies — he chose to remain in that office and I started my progression in the second position.

The installation ceremony was held at a local restaurant, and a Toastmaster by the name of Durwood English served as the installing officer. He was a member of the International Board of Directors who would be elected International President in 1977. During the social time that followed, Durwood came up to me and said, "I've never installed a woman in a Toastmasters office and I'm not sure I like doing it."

This took me by surprise. To this point, I had been sheltered among supportive members in my local club and I have never forgotten that first encounter with someone who was not especially pleased to have a woman in the organization. Nonetheless, I have always given Durwood credit for being very diplomatic in expressing his opposition. Before long, this attitude mellowed as I earned his approval and we developed a friendship that included his wife, Mary.

A short time after I became a member, my Toastmasters involvement began to give me visibility. As it happened, the captain and the technical director requested a briefing on one of the Center's projects each week. When the FORACS Project team was asked to brief the Center's military and civilian commanding officers, our supervisor called a meeting.

"Who would like to give the briefing?" he asked. Not one hand went up. He looked around and then focused on me. "Helen, you're a Toastmaster. Why don't you tell them about the data bank?"

"Okay," I managed to reply. Since I was the lowest grade-level in the room, I was surprised to be given this responsibility.

I had a week to develop this briefing and I put everything I'd learned in Toastmasters to work. My briefing organization would follow the Toastmasters speech format with an opening, body and conclusion. I would introduce my subject, present the information in a logical order, and conclude with a summarization of all I had said. I practiced using effective gestures and voice projection plus I worked hard to avoid those pesky filler words. I also gave some thought to the questions that might be asked and prepared myself to respond. My past experience in making charts and graphs for reports came in handy, as I prepared overhead transparencies to illustrate my briefing with visuals. If PowerPoint had been around back then, there's no doubt I would have worked with it.

The day finally came and the briefing went as well as I'd hoped. The captain and technical director asked questions and expressed surprise that more projects in the Center weren't making use of the data we had accumulated in the bank. They said they would recommend its use to other departments. Needless to say, my supervisor was pleased. After that, whenever I met the captain or technical director in the hallways of the main building, they greeted me with a nod and a curt, "Helen." At my grade-level, and one of about 1500 employees,

instant recognition by Command personnel was fairly rare. I
had the Toastmaster program to thank for this bonus.

Earlier I described Andros as the least developed island in the
Bahamas and the austere life it offered its tenants. Later, however, in the spring of 1971 I was exposed to the advantages of
living on an undeveloped island where boating is one of the
few pleasures. One of the engineers and his wife invited me
for a sail aboard their trimaran. That evening we sailed up the
coast of Andros and pulled into a cove on the northern coast
as the sun was sinking toward the west. We relaxed on deck
with a drink while steaks sizzled on the grill. We enjoyed a
delicious dinner at dusk then motored back to the range under
a full moon. The beautiful waters of the Caribbean and the
splendid twilight embracing the island offered an exquisite
setting for our sail.

When I returned home, I raved to John about my sailing
experience. He was thrilled and immediately signed us up
for sailing lessons. I was surprised to learn that he had always wanted to sail. We spent the next weekend training on
a small boat, and I had my first taste of sailing as a member
of the crew—I was almost knocked overboard by the boom
twice and every muscle in my body ached for weeks afterward. When we finally completed the course, I qualified as
first mate—the one who dodges the boom—and John qualified as captain. We joined the Navy Sailing Club. Membership
included boat rental privileges, and we enjoyed many sails on
San Diego Bay.

At this stage of our lives, John and I could spend more
time together—our children were leaving the nest. Bruce
was attending nearby San Diego State University. He began

experimenting with living away from home. After the first semester of college, he moved to the dorm for a while. Then, for a while, he moved back home. Cheryl graduated high school with plans to be married and move to Florida. I was sad to see her go so far away. She was so thrilled about getting married that I couldn't help but remember the whirlwind romance John and I experienced and the joy of our wedding. Along with my sadness at seeing her go, I had to share some of her happiness.

That summer, John and I celebrated our 25th wedding anniversary. He took me to the Hotel del Coronado — a striking white hotel on the sands of Coronado Bay — and we ate in an especially beautiful part of this San Diego historical landmark known as the Prince of Wales Room. It was a romantic treat for a very special day that I will never forget.

By this time the FORACS Project had grown: more ranges were added, more tests were being conducted and the data bank had become an integral part of the program. In midsummer, I was given the responsibility for all the software used at all the ranges and named head of the Data Bank Section.

I don't remember how many people were employed in the section in the beginning. The core personnel included Jim Dyer, Stan Miyamoto, Joan Ainsworth, Joan Sieber and Betty Zonkel filling positions as an electronic engineer, a computer operator, two math technicians and a tech aid. Temporary workers were used to augment this group when needed. Our group turned out to be a good working and socializing mix and we enjoyed a long and lasting circle of friendship that extended into our retirement years.

I worked with the data bank from its inception, putting it into operation and introduced methods of uniform data processing to the ranges. Although I received credit for managing the data

Blanchard Collection

On our 25th wedding anniversary, John took me to dinner in the Prince of Wales
Room at the Hotel Del Coronado in San Diego.

bank, two others played a very significant role in its creation
and success. The data bank was the brainchild of Chuck Sturte-
vant in the Analysis Group and Willie de la Houssaye was the
main programmer.

In September, I made my second visit to the FORACS range
on Cape Cod. The weather was much better than the unsea-
sonably heavy snow that occurred during my previous visit in
1967. Also, the range manager and I were better acquainted
and far more comfortable in our professional positions. This
time, I received a warm welcome, and he invited me to his
home for a lovely dinner with his wife and family.

While on the East Coast, I took a few days annual leave for a
visit with my sister Vlasta and her family in Pennsylvania.

When I arrived back at the Center I found an invitation to the Woman of the Year presentation awaiting me along with a request that I attend. The formal announcement was supposed to surprise the recipient. However, word leaked out and I knew that I was the Center's Woman of the year before the event. Still, to say I was thrilled is an understatement.

I had been honored with a nomination the previous year and received a consolation letter after someone else won from Captain Van Orden, the commanding officer of the Center. This letter was filled with praise and humbled me with the words, "Your nomination reflects your exemplary work performance…and technical endeavor expected of not only women but all employees in the Federal government." To receive the Woman of the Year Award in 1971 was a great honor and very special to me.

I received an engraved plaque and desk pen set at a ceremony held in the Cloud Room adjacent to the cafeteria in the Center. All the Center's personnel were encouraged to attend and guest and family members were invited, as well. Cheryl was in Florida and couldn't come. But Bruce, John and his mother Naudine were there.

After the award ceremony, all the women at the Center were invited to a coffee at the captain's home on the base. First Lady Pat Nixon sent a special greeting to all the women at the Center and it was presented to me at the party. This day was one of the highlights of my career. A feature article with my photo appeared in the *Calendar* describing my work with the FORACS Data Bank, the San Diego Union also covered the story, and I received many letters of congratulations.

That fall, John and I enjoyed a vacation — just the two of us. We drove up the coast for a leisurely sightseeing tour of Solvang, Morrow Bay, Hearst Castle, Carmel by the Sea, and San Francisco. Then we turned inland toward Eureka and Reno before

Courtesy Space and Naval Warfare Systems San Diego

Captain Van Orden presented me with the Center's Woman of the Year Award in 1971.

heading back to San Diego. It was a delightful trip, a wonderful time together, and a rare indulgence for us. I only recall two family trips while we were raising our children. When they were younger, we were a Navy family, moving often and too short of cash most years to plan a pleasure trip. After we settled in Allied Gardens and built the pool, our backyard — a gathering place for teens, neighbors and colleagues from work — was just too inviting to leave in the summer.

At the Toastmasters International Convention in August of 1971, an amendment to allow women in Toastmasters was brought to a vote. It was rejected. After this rejection, Bob Bolan requested permission for our club to include women in its membership since we were sponsored by the Center and meeting on Federal property. As a result, in November 1971, while I was finishing my term as club secretary, we received a memo from the Executive Director granting us permission to change our by-laws to admit women. In January of 1972, Homer was removed from our membership roll, and our club nominated and elected Helen Blanchard as vice president membership.

Enthusiastically accepting the challenge of expanding our membership, I began to think of a way to use two members who were close friends and highly competitive. I asked them each to form a team and compete against each other in recruiting new members. A club dinner provided the prize, steak for the winners and beans for the losers. This ignited a fire and in just one month we gained 12 new members. Our club was growing so fast that the vice president education asked us to slow down so he could catch up on the assignments for Ice Breaker speeches! During this membership drive I invited our captain to attend a club meeting. Without a doubt, his show of support contributed to the membership gain as well as the friendly competition.

May brought another flurry of activity with another week-long manager training course in San Francisco followed by a quick celebration of Mother's Day and my 46th birthday before a trip to Hawaii. In June I was off to Andros Island to visit the AUTEC range again. On this trip I was scheduled to observe a test aboard the destroyer escort USS McCandless DE-1084. This would be my first time aboard a ship on the range and my first time aboard a large ship since we sailed to Brazil aboard the SS Argentina. I could almost feel myself pale just remembering those swells off the coast of the Carolinas.

Armed with seasick pills and filled with dread, I forced myself to go. What if I embarrassed myself by making a really bad presentation while on board? As it turned out, the "Tongue of the Ocean" — the testing area — was as smooth as glass and I didn't feel the least bit queasy. Fear of seasickness was not my only concern. Once again, I was probably the first woman to enter this area of man's territory. My apprehension was completely unfounded. I was welcomed aboard, and a young sailor gave a tour of the ship as he escorted me to the sonar area. When we visited the bridge, the captain asked if I would like to sit in his chair.

"Sure would!" I said. And I did.

That July, upon return to the Center and Toastmasters, I was elected vice president education. This was the last progressive step in club leadership positions before becoming president of the Center's Toastmaster's Club 2539.

A few months later, I became a member of Federally Employed Women (FEW). This was my first involvement in any organization that sought equal opportunity for women. I was never an activist in the women's movement but became involved in FEW to help promote equal opportunity for women at the Center.

This organization hoped to attain its objectives by suggestion and educational means aimed at top management. We worked to call attention to the discrimination in the workforce: typically women were classified a grade lower than men doing the same work. Very often upper management — those in positions to make meaningful changes — were not aware of this practice. We also made a request that women be given opportunities to serve on committees and, probably most important, we asked for equality in training opportunities.

I knew the value of training programs better than most — not from wishing for them but from receiving the same training opportunities as the men in the FORACS group. Many women were stuck in dead-end jobs because, for one reason or another, sometimes just the way the system worked, they did not receive training.

I was one of nine selected to serve on the Center's Junior Executive Board. This group was set up to assist the Senior Executive board by making recommendations for possible solutions to the items on their agenda concerning policy and people problems. It was an honor to be a member of this group, and in this role I was in a position to call attention to the problems that involved inequality and women at the Center.

This was a full and exciting year in my life. I was about to become president of our local club and I could go into this leadership position full of enthusiasm for what Toastmasters had done for me. I am certain that Toastmasters is a career booster. In December 1972, my boss recommended me for a promotion to GS-12. A month later, I received the "12" and the head of personnel at the Center called me in and told me that this was the end of the line.

"Don't even think of a higher grade," she said. Her negative attitude denied me the positive thoughts I should have been enjoying. Instead, I felt unjustly admonished.

I had never asked for a promotion — in every case, my superiors had made the recommendations without any input from me. The good news? She was wrong. This wasn't the end of the line for me.

Chapter 8

Bittersweet Year

1973 arrived with a flourish that promised good times ahead and everything seemed right with my world. As is often the case, however, good times ebb and flow and changes can come suddenly. This year would leave me with bittersweet memories.

By the time my GS-12 promotion kicked off the year, John's negative attitude toward women in the workplace had mellowed. In fact, he beamed when he heard my good news. John loved entertaining, and his first thought was to host a celebration. My feelings didn't match his enthusiasm. I wasn't sure that I wanted a party.

"I don't know..." I murmured, shaking my head, trying to discourage him.

But John wouldn't be swayed. He insisted that my upgrade was "something to be proud of—something to celebrate."

I had to admit, it was a definite high point. I started at the Center as a GS-4 bookkeeping machine operator and in eleven years, I had reached the GS-12 level. Of course I was proud...but in my own way. However, it was a lot of fun when John carried through with his plans for a celebration. He reserved a room at the Chief Petty Officers Club at the Naval Training Center and

invited my coworkers to a cocktail party. About 20 people attended and we had a very pleasant evening.

That same month, I enjoyed another memorable event — my
election and installation as president of the Center's Toastmasters Club. The installation ceremony and dinner took place at
the King's Inn in Mission Valley, in the heart of San Diego's
Hotel Circle. Most of our members brought guests along to
take part in the festivities. And for me, it was most special to
see the pride in the eyes of the men closest to me in life, my
husband and son. John and Bruce escorted me to the event
and shared my sense of accomplishment — my happiness — on
that special evening.

Newly-elected club president, Helen Blanchard with incoming officers: Earl
Floren, Bob Crittenden, Pat Johnson, Anthony Louie, and Russ Eyres.

During my six-month term, I oversaw a very capable group
of officers in a well-maintained club with supportive members.
My goals included increasing the membership and promoting

Toastmasters at the Center. I wanted others to have the opportunity to benefit as I had. My belief in Toastmasters remains strong: the Toastmaster experience offers more than improved communication skills. Club officers receive valuable management training and the opportunity to gain leadership experience. And so, I was convinced that the growth of Toastmasters at the Center, possibly adding another club, would benefit the Center as well as individual employees.

Soon after I became president of my local club, I attended the District 5 High School Speech Contest. The contestants were winners of contests sponsored by Toastmaster clubs at high schools within the district. Since District 5 included San Diego and Imperial Counties in Southern California plus Yuma, Arizona and Baja California in Mexico, this was a large competition. I was so impressed with these young people as they stood before the audience, spoke with confidence, and expressed themselves well.

Toastmasters' first President, J. Clark Chamberlain, had established this program in District 5 and it continued to be an annual event. He was still active in Toastmasters at the time and attended this contest. This was my first glimpse of this renowned Toastmaster.

J. Clark Chamberlain had played an important role in Toastmasters history. The idea for Toastmasters came from a man named Ralph Smedley, who worked at the Young Men's Christian Association (YMCA). He created a program to help young men overcome their fear of public speaking, and over a twenty-year period he organized clubs in four cities. Unfortunately, each club folded soon after Smedley moved on to his next YMCA assignment.

J. Clark Chamberlain visited the last club that Smedley had organized in Santa Ana, California. Impressed with the idea,

Chamberlain asked for—and was granted—permission to start a similar club in Anaheim. The idea spread and five other clubs sprang to life in Orange County. J. Clark had helped Smedley achieve a critical mass in public awareness and membership that sparked the initial growth of Toastmasters.

Sometime after that, he came to San Diego and started Club No. 7. The first club outside California was chartered in 1933 and Toastmasters crossed the U.S. border into British Columbia with a club chartered in Victoria in 1935. Growth continued at a steady pace and by June 2004, Toastmasters International had chartered its 10,000th club and the membership grew to more than 225,000 people.

In the early days of Toastmasters, Ralph Smedley was known as the "Creator of the Toastmaster Idea" and J. Clark was known as the "Organizer and President." Later, however, J. Clark's involvement faded from the public's memory.

In the early 1970s, I was always on the lookout for education and training opportunities and, naturally, the announcement of a seminar for career women on transactional analysis caught my attention. This was the first training seminar I had seen for career women and I wanted to attend. My supervisor approved my request and I was off to San Francisco in early March.

This proved to be a new experience for me—for the first time, I wasn't in the minority. The course emphasized understanding behavior. We were made aware of how we reacted to others in certain situations and how they might react to us. We were asked to ponder the direction we were going in our careers, set a goal, and determine the changes we would need to make to reach that goal. I am not sure I set any grand goal at the time. Nevertheless, much of what I learned at that seminar affected how I thought about my future and how I would proceed, one step at a time, as opportunities came my way.

Soon after attending the seminar, I visited the AUTEC range again. The Bahamas were about to be granted Independence. But the islands were still part of the United Kingdom at that time and the United States and the U.K. shared this range. I had made plans to observe a British ship on the range and discuss the possibility of a U.K. data bank.

The HMS Minerva, a Royal Navy Leander-class frigate, happened to be scheduled for the range at a time I could get away from the Center. A couple of days before I left San Diego, I received a call from the range manager saying they might have a surprise for me; Prince Charles, heir to the British throne, might be aboard. This information would have had me shaking in my boots if it hadn't been for those Thursday meetings I'd spent with Toastmasters.

The dockside preparation for the test was held in the city of Freeport on the Grand Bahama Island. Even at the time, Freeport was a bustling tourist city (nothing like Andros Island) with an elegant casino, a colorful marketplace, lovely hotels, fine restaurants and stage shows. One evening, several members of our group decided to take advantage of the nightlife and see a show at the Holiday Inn featuring the comedian Redd Foxx. They invited me, and I went along not knowing what to expect. I have to admit, I was disappointed. While the others laughed, I missed the point of what seemed to be the funniest jokes. When I returned home to San Diego, later, I told John about the show and repeated some of the jokes I'd heard. His reaction surprised me. I had never seen an old Navy man blush like that! He told me never, never to repeat those words again.

While the Minerva was in Freeport's harbor, I went aboard to observe the dockside phase of the tests which included briefing the ship's crew about the on-range test procedures, preparation and staffing requirements.

The British liaison officer took charge of the introductions and when he came to me, I was astonished to hear, "Mrs. Helen Blanchard of the Navy Electronics Laboratory Center in California who will give us a brief description of the Center's involvement in FORACS."

Had this happened two or three years earlier, I would have been completely speechless. Thanks to Toastmasters Table Topic experience, I stepped forward with confidence and delivered the requested impromptu briefing.

When I finished, the British Liaison Officer said, "Jolly well done, you know."

Later that day, the captain of the Minerva apologized because he hadn't received permission for me to board the ship on-range. He explained that authorization from the Minister of War, in London, was necessary since women were not allowed aboard a British Man of War on the high seas. The Tongue of the Ocean is hardly "high seas" but all rules had to be followed. I left with no expectation of being allowed back aboard for the test scheduled in two days.

However, a wire from London arrived at the last minute and the morning of the test, I found myself aboard a small boat preparing to rendezvous with the Minerva at 0700 in the Tongue of the Ocean.

I had a delightful day aboard. I found the British to be gracious hosts and Prince Charles, indeed, was on board. I was on the bridge watching the crew rig the Grimes Light on the Jack staff for the on-range test when Prince Charles strolled out on deck.

The Officer of the Day said, "I say, look at the chap. Walks just like his father, you know, hands behind his back." About

Blanchard Collection

Helen Blanchard enjoying a photo op beside the British frigate, H.M.S. Minerva while the ship was undergoing FORACS testing procedures.

that time, Prince Charles looked up at the light. "Probably wondering what that blinking light is doing on the deck of his ship," the officer added and explained that the prince had a wonderful sense of humor.

I could tell that Prince Charles was admired and well-liked. I saw him several times during the day. He was the ship's navigator and, although he spent much of his time in the chart room, he did walk about the deck with a sextant in his hand and came to the bridge several times to confer with the captain.

Later, our group gathered in the Ward Room for lunch and chatted about the coming independence for the Bahamas scheduled for July 10th. I still enjoy a delightful memory of suddenly becoming aware that the prince had entered the room unnoticed.

"Not a new experience; we've had this happen with the Colonies before, you know," he chimed in. We could hear the humor in his voice and as he nodded at our group of Americans — former colonists — we couldn't miss the twinkle in his eye.

My six-month term as club president ended about that time. As I left office, I complained to Bob Bolam about the ineffectiveness of our area governor during this time. The person in this position serves as advisor to several clubs in the district. I had never met ours and did not receive any advice or direction during my term.

Bob suggested that I take that position for the next term — area governor was an appointed position at the district level. After realizing that I was interested, I am sure that Bob told the then district governor that I would serve if I were asked. There was no competition for positions at this level and I was offered the appointment.

Of course, I talked to John before accepting, and he encouraged me to continue my involvement with Toastmasters. I accepted the position thinking this would be my last position on the Toastmasters leadership ladder. John went with me to the District 5 installation event at the Hanalei Restaurant in Mission Valley.

San Diego Mayor Pete Wilson was the guest speaker. An interesting man, Pete Wilson had served in the California Assembly before becoming Mayor. From the San Diego Mayor's office, he moved up to the U.S. Senate and then returned to California to be elected our state's governor.

A few weeks later, John went with me to the Region II Conference in Long Beach, California. The conference was held aboard the Queen Mary. The luxurious ocean-liner had been converted to a tourist attraction, complete with hotel and convention center. We had a cabin aboard the permanently docked vessel and reminisced about the first time we were aboard a ship together — our trip to Rio de Janeiro. These memories rekindled our shipboard romance, and we shared a delightful time in Long Beach.

Soon after attending that conference, I began fulfilling my role as area governor. I reserved a meeting room at the Center and arranged a training event for the six clubs I had been given to nurture. Determined to give these clubs all the support I could, I solicited the help of experienced Toastmasters. They prepared briefs on the duties of each office and presented information on setting goals and planning meetings. The event was a well-received success.

In August I missed the Toastmaster International Convention in Houston. At that time, I was on travel for the Center and could not attend. The FORACS II range was being moved from Guantanamo, and I was a member of a training team sent to the new location on Vieques Island off the coast of Puerto Rico. While I was busy training the new FORACS personnel at this range, a major change was being considered in Houston at the Convention. A resolution came to a vote — and passed — that allowed clubs the option of changing their by-laws to admit women. This was a non-aggressive, gentle way to open the organization to women without forcing everyone to comply. Clubs with a membership that opposed the coed atmosphere could leave their by-laws unchanged and remain all-male. Now that the door was officially open, more women joined the clubs that welcomed them, and in the following years, the number of coed clubs gradually increased. Later, by Federal decree, all clubs were forced to admit women.

In the fall, I received the Outstanding Toastmaster Award from the Center's Toastmasters Club. The new club president,

Bob Crittenden, presented me with a trophy and recognized me for my "efforts and dedication to Toastmaster principles." The recipient of annual award was selected based on a system where members accumulate points for speaking skills, evaluation techniques, recruiting, and participation in internal and external Toastmaster events.

In late September and early October, John and I topped off an eventful and thrilling year with a vacation in the beautiful New England area. We flew to Boston, rented a car and began a drive through the Northeast where autumn arrives with a burst of brilliant colors. We visited good friends in Massachusetts, drove up the coast of Maine, turned inland toward Quebec, Canada, then headed south through Vermont at the peak of the fall foliage season. We found memorable breathtaking scenes around every corner.

A few weeks after we returned to San Diego, John suffered another heart attack and spent several days in the hospital undergoing tests. He had been released and was home when his doctor called us to his office to discuss the test results. I sat in shock as he told us that there was nothing he could prescribe that would make John's heart stronger or restore the damaged tissue. The old heart was beyond repair and John needed a new one. This was 1973 and heart transplantation was still in the experimental stage. Human hearts had been successfully transplanted but this was a case where the surgery was successful and the patient died. Transplant surgeons could replace organs but they could not prevent rejection. Thus, a new heart was not an option.

John asked the doctor to be truthful, "How long?" he wanted to know.

"Six months," came the dreadful response. Then he went on to explain that the six month prognosis could be extended if

John changed his lifestyle, limited his activity, and existed as an invalid. He talked about "quantity of life versus quality of life."

I knew what John's choice would be without hearing the words. He was a person who would either live a full life... or not live at all.

John was John. He loved to entertain and a damaged heart was not going to change that. FORACS hosted a range managers' meeting in San Diego late in November and he insisted that we entertain the group in our home. He participated and enjoyed every minute of it. A few weeks later he went on disability retirement and his group gave him a farewell luncheon five days before Christmas. No one in the group knew the prognosis. But everyone knew that a forced retirement because of a heart problem did not portend a long, happy time in one's golden years. John enjoyed a strong bond with his co-workers and although no one had been told, everyone knew he didn't have long.

I was determined to keep a smile on my face. I expected this to be my most difficult "presentation." Yet, I should have known that John would use his sense of humor to keep the atmosphere light and fill the room with laughter.

In San Diego, December skies may be blue and sunny or filled with gray clouds that bring drizzle. That is how our life was as the year came to an end. John and I shared a quiet and thoughtful Christmas season. We counted our blessings and hoped for more time together.

Chapter 9

On the Campaign Trail

After the holidays we began adjusting to our new routine, with John staying home while I went to work. Each moment became precious as we lived our days with hope tempered in reality, and in the beginning — conflicting opinions.

I nagged and pleaded with John to curtail some of his activities. John, however, wanted to enjoy whatever time he had left to the fullest. This meant that he would continue building his hydroponic greenhouse, and if he wanted to plant a tree he would dig a hole in our hard, rocky soil. This soon led to a heart-to-heart discussion where John reminded me that *quality of life* was extremely important to him. I had to respect his wishes, outwardly, at least. John also wanted me to have a full life and encouraged me to meet all the demands of my job at the Center and enjoy my Toastmasters activities.

With six months remaining in my one year term as area governor, I kept the schedule I had originally set. That January, I held another training session for newly-elected club officers and another speech contest in April. I planned and organized these events from beginning to end including creating and distributing flyers, making reservations, and collecting fees — plus scheduling speakers for the training session and judges for the contest. Both events came off without a hitch and I was pleased with the turnout and enjoyed that good feeling of accomplishment.

In April, Bob Bolam suggested that I run for the entry-level office in District 5: lieutenant (lt.) governor organization. This was an elected position and third from the top in the district hierarchy. This elected officer was responsible for training and guidance of the eight area governors. John and I discussed this, and he urged me to campaign for this position. He said that he knew how much I thought of this organization and enjoyed working for it. He volunteered to help and, of course, he began planning a party.

The Saturday before the District 5 Spring Conference, John invited friends and Toastmasters supporters to a "Poster Painting Patio Party." Bob supplied white shelf paper, poster paint and brushes. John added humor and food and everyone tried their hand at designing creative "Vote for Helen" posters. John contributed the best slogan: "She's Not a 'MS' — She's a HIT!"

The party injected enthusiasm into my campaign, and just as John planned, we accomplished a lot while having a great time.

A week later, we were ready for the big day at the district conference. John and Bruce added "Vote for Helen" banners and posters to the colorful array that filled the hall. My supporters and I wore campaign buttons and mingled in the crowd. In this atmosphere, it was easy to ask for votes. My competitors conducted tough campaigns with the help of their dedicated supporters. They were working the crowd, too. But when the vote was counted that afternoon, they had elected me.

I was elated! John and Bruce shared my enthusiasm. The excitement of winning and thoughts of taking on new challenges offered me a bright spot in a time filled with worry. I couldn't

John organized a poster painting party on our patio. His slogan, "She's Not a 'MS' – She's a HIT!" was the best.

wait to tackle this new job. I knew the newly-appointed area governors (all male) from past Toastmasters events. They were dedicated Toastmasters and would welcome training and guidance from the lt. governor organization. By this time, I no longer held the distinction of "lone woman" in the district office. Women were serving in two appointed positions: publicity chairman and assistant publicity chairman.

John and I moved ahead, living life as normally as we could. Inside I worried while John continued with the activities of his choice. On June 21st, he invited Bruce over for the afternoon. I arrived home to find that they had scrubbed and waxed our big family room floor. John looked a little tired, and I was concerned that he might have overexerted. Feeling apprehensive, I decided to cancel my plans for the evening and stay home. John assured me that he was feeling fine and urged me to go. I argued, but he insisted. So, reluctantly, I dressed. John took my photo as I went out the door on my way to the Toastmasters event — we were chartering a new club that evening. It was a special evening with a Hawaiian theme.

After the meeting, a group of Toastmasters friends invited me to join them for a social time. Normally, I would have stayed but I had a strong desire to go home. When I arrived John seemed fine. He had been watching a movie, and offered to fix me a drink while I changed into something more comfortable than my Hawaiian outfit. Then I joined him and we shared the events of the evening; his movie and my meeting. He was relaxed in his favorite chair, drinking a beer and eating potato chips while our two Siamese cats purred in his lap — and suddenly, I was calling 911!

In an instant, John had suffered a massive heart attack. Although they pronounced him dead at the hospital, I am sure he was gone before the paramedics arrived. He was just 53 years old.

I will always be grateful that I felt that urge to go home that evening and we had those last few minutes together. My reactions to his death and ultimately my life would have been so different if he had died while I was away. I would never have continued my Toastmasters involvement. But, God blessed me by allowing me to be there, and I know — with the assurance of our family doctor — there was absolutely nothing I could have done to save my beloved husband.

I was not alone for long. Bruce lived in San Diego. He rushed to me, Cheryl flew home from Florida, family came from the Midwest, and friends called and visited. Carrying out John's wishes, we scattered his ashes at sea and there was no service. The flood of sympathy cards and letters gave the children and me comfort and made us realize how many people knew and respected this man. Still, it was, without doubt, the most difficult time in my life.

My doctor said, "Go back to work" — and I did. Dedicating all my energy to work and Toastmasters left me little idle time and helped me through the grieving process.

During this time, I devoted countless hours to the Toastmasters program. I accepted numerous guest speaker invitations and attended all the area events, parties and district council meetings plus the district conference. The International Convention was held at the Disneyland Hotel in Anaheim that August and I attended this annual event for the first time. Durwood English was running for 3rd vice president that summer and I joined the others from our district in campaigning for him. Wearing Durwood's campaign button on my jacket, I mingled with Toastmasters from all over the world, shaking hands, chatting, and making new friends. I thoroughly enjoyed this campaign experience. Durwood won the election, and three years later he became President of Toastmasters International.

I didn't make any FORACS trips in 1974, but that September the Center invited a group of NATO representatives to a meeting in San Diego to discuss the possible establishment of NATO FORACS ranges. The Captain of the Center hosted a cocktail party at his home for all those attending the meeting, including representatives from the U.K., Denmark, Norway, Germany, Italy, Greece and France. As a member of the U.S. team, I was invited and delighted to attend. I met many new people and reconnected with the representative from the U.K. who I knew from my AUTEC visits. I enjoyed seeing him again and meeting his wife.

This was an exciting time as FORACS was about to expand to Europe and I was involved. I thought the double crown prophesy had been fulfilled with my Navy wife voyage to South America and my trips to offshore FORACS ranges. In the near future, however, the prophesy would be fulfilled in the way it was envisioned at the time of my birth. I would be crossing the Atlantic.

A few weeks later, the FORACS assignments were realigned and the Data Bank Section responsibility was expanded to include the development, maintenance and quality control of all FORACS computer software plus responsibility and operational control of the Project Office computer system. Our expanded Data Bank Section became a branch known as Code 6901 under the organizational system at the Center. The workload increased in Code 6901 and I hired additional workers. The expanded operation took my full attention leaving no idle time at work, and Toastmasters filled most of my leisure hours.

My busy schedule helped me through the first few months without John but thoughts of the coming holiday season filled me with dread. The pain was too new for the bright lights and cheerful greetings to stir memories, and I expected a December filled with a sense of overwhelming loss and loneliness. Instead, I found myself surrounded by family and close friends. Dad and Irene arrived mid-December for Christmas in San Diego and John's mother and Bruce lived nearby. Close friends and neighbors dropped by often. These people, so dear to my heart, shared my loss and the phrase, "tidings of comfort and joy," took on a new meaning.

After Christmas, encouraged by the memory of John's love for entertaining and celebration — I took a firm grip on my new life — and hosted a New Year's Eve party. I invited the

Code 6901 group, along with friends and family. My party-hostess debut seemed to be a fitting way to usher in the New Year and celebrate my survival of the first holiday season in 28 years without John.

I followed up with an old-fashioned Nebraska farm-days pinochle party for Dad and Irene. This party set a precedent although few of my invited guests had Nebraska farm roots. Players who had learned to play in the military shared a love for the game with the old farmers. Pinochle players from the Center soon learned that when Dad and Irene arrived each year, a pinochle party was soon to follow.

My climb to the first level of district leadership had gone smoothly. No one I knew seemed to mind that a woman had been elected to this office. I was feeling good about my Toast-masters experience and thinking positive thoughts about my campaign for lt. governor education when a missing rung jeopardized my climb up the Toastmasters leadership ladder. I discovered that some old-timers who had occupied the top rungs of that ladder were not pleased to have women partici-pating in their organization.

By 1975, J. Clark Chamberlain had been involved in Toast-masters just over 50 years. He had served as the first President of Toastmasters, was active in Club No. 7 in San Diego with a continuing interest in the district and International program. Every year he invited the top three District 5 officers to the San Diego Club No. 7 to give a district status report. Since I was the lt. governor organization, I expected to attend along with the lt. governor education and governor. Chamberlain's club cel-ebrated its 45th anniversary that year. Before I had time to buy my new dress for this special occasion, Club No. 7's president called to tell me that J. Clark did not approve of women in the organization and therefore I was not welcome to attend.

I was stunned and I had no intention of going where I was not wanted. So, I accepted this disappointing news and erased that entry from my appointment book.

A few days later, I received a call from Durwood English, International 2nd Vice President at the time. "Are you ready for the big event?" he asked.

"No." I said and then explained about the distressing call I'd received.

Durwood responded quickly, "You have to go." Sometime later, I heard that Durwood called J. Clark and told him that he had to accept the fact that women were now in the organization and that all the district officers would be attending. I went — but reluctantly. I didn't know what to expect or the extent of the hostility I might face.

That evening I found that there was a plan in place. When I arrived at the Mission Valley Inn, my mentor, Bob Bolam met me at my car and escorted me into the private meeting room where I felt very conspicuous as the only woman in this gathering of Toastmasters elites. Friends awaited us at the reception table. They surrounded me and we all sat together at a table near the door. I was ignored during the program — but I was there, representing my office and the district.

The next April, I was serving as lt. governor education for District 5 and I received notice of Club No. 7's annual event with a handwritten note from J. Clark at the bottom asking me to attend as "his guest." I was quite pleased to receive his invitation and I accepted. J. Clark paid for my meal and, once again, I was the only woman present.

A year later, I was district governor and my announcement came with a personal handwritten note. This time he wrote,

"Dear Helen, I hope you are available to 'decorate' our Head Table…"

Then, a few months later, after I completed my term as governor of District 5, I received the following letter from J. Clark. Over the years, I have cherished this letter and I have often mentioned it in my speeches.

Community Christmas Center Committee

J. Clark Chamberlain, Chairman
Energy Products and Services Assoc.

Chandler Bach, Vice Chairman
Cheverton-Bach, Bayly, Martin & Fay

George I. Loveland, Secretary
Park and Recreation Department
Casa del Prado
San Diego, California 92101
Telephone: 236-5984

MEMBERS

THOMAS ALLAN
Salvation Army

PAUL BROWN
Security Mutual Life

NANCY COATE
Rehabilitation Center
San Diego State University

DOUGLAS IAN DUNCAN
S. D. Civic Organist

LESTER E. EARNEST
Former Park & Recreation Director
City of San Diego

LYLE EARNEST
Bank of America

DR. CHARLES FREEBERN
San Diego
Unified School District

ALBERT GABBS
Gabbs Store Equipment

CAPT. C. M. HERDERING
U. S. Marine Corps

HELEN LENYK
Cabrillo International
Folk Dance Club

DR. FRANK LOWE
Retired

RUTH PEARSON
House of Pacific Relations

PAUL SCHMIDT
Sun Harbor Chorus
S.P.E.B.S.Q.S.A.

DR. C. RICHARD SHANOR
Metro United Methodist Urban Ministry

MR. & MRS. RUDOLPH VARGAS
Vargas Studios
Los Angeles, California

San Diego, California
July 11, 1977

Helen Blanchard DTM
Immediate Past Governor
District Five
TOASTMASTERS INTERNATIONAL

In view of my strong original opposition to women in Toastmasters, you might assume this letter would be a difficult one to write. Far from it. What you have done for us as our Governor during the past year, and in fact during your entire career as a Toastmaster, certainly changed my views.

You must have realized long before now, that in my position as the principal organizer and the First President of TOASTMASTERS INTERNATION from 1930 to 1932, that the acceptance of women was difficult for me. Now, you personnaly Helen, have changed this for me. Women Members are a reality, and their numbers are increasing rapidly. They are entitled to representation surely, and you are the one to "break the Ice".

Having worked with every Governor since District Five came into being, I can testify that you have been the most effective Chief Executive we have ever had, even though all those of recent years have been unusually succesful. You are not just a very attractive woman with an exceptional facility in public speaking. You have become a true Leader not only in your own District, but throughout the Region.

All who have worked with you recognized your organizational and management talents early in the game and have enthusiastically joined in your efforts on behalf of all of us. Outstanding Ability, no matter whether possessed by a man or woman, seems to generate great support on the part of others involved in the same movement.

Because of the highly classified nature of your extensive responsibilities at the Naval Electronics Laboratories, very little can be known of what you do. All we of District Five know, is that your Organizational and Management knowhow has been great for us. It will be great for Toastmasters everywhere, when you become the the first woman to serve as a Member of the Board of Directors.

J. Clark Chamberlain

4224 Adams Avenue
San Diego, 92116

Sponsored by the City of San Diego Park and Recreation Department, Ed Mendoza, Director

Printed with the permission of Joseph McCulley, grandson and next of kin to J. Clark Chamberlain.

After I completed my term as governor of District 5, I received this letter from J. Clark Chamberlain.

In 1975, as I set my sights on winning the race for lt. governor education, I entered stiff competition. My worthy opponent wanted the position as much as I did, and I knew he would run an excellent campaign. In the six weeks preceding the district conference, I put in a maximum effort. In addition to my work at the Center, I visited 34 clubs, attended eight area speech contests, and one council meeting. It seemed that I shook hands and smiled continuously for six weeks. A few days before the conference, I wrapped the campaign up John style with a poster painting party. Like the year before, the conference hall was filled with colorful banners, and each candidate and their supporters worked the floor for votes. When the count was in that day in May, 1975, I won.

About this time, Terry McCann became Executive Director of Toastmasters International. He served in this position from March 1975 until he retired in 2001. Terry joined Toastmasters after winning the gold medal for wrestling in the 1960 Olympics in Rome. As he gained fame in the National and International Wrestling Hall of Fame, he received many speaking invitations. Although he didn't lack confidence (as I had), he soon realized that he was not reaching his audience.

He is quoted as saying, "I couldn't figure out why people weren't excited about my 150 slides of me wrestling."

A friend pointed him toward a local Toastmasters club. After gaining communications skills through the program, Terry built a career in advertising and association management, reaching his zenith as Executive Director for Toastmasters International.

While most of my time that summer was devoted to Toastmasters and my job at the Center, my personal life held some demands, too. My daughter had divorced shortly before John's death. She moved back to San Diego and remarried in May of 1975.

About that time, I decided to move to a new home. On June 21, with one year of widowhood behind me, I packed my belongings and memories, left Allied Gardens, and moved to a Point Loma condo much closer to the Center. In doing so, I exchanged the big family room, backyard pool, and entertainment patio for a view of sailboats on San Diego Bay and frequent walks on the sandy beach. Thanks to Toastmasters and the Center, my first year without John went by fairly fast — and I survived.

As that milestone slipped into the past, my activity level continued at a steady pace. On June 22, after one night in my new condo, I boarded a plane bound for Hawaii and our Toastmasters Region II Conference. Then upon returning to San Diego, I had a few weeks to unpack and settle in while I conducted a Youth Leadership Program at the Center for the summer aides. The eight-week program in the fundamentals of communication and leadership in addition to my regular duties overloaded my weekdays but still left the weekends free for relaxation as well as Toastmasters activities.

In August, I attended the International Convention in Washington D.C. where our district earned the President's Distinguished District Award. The governors of the districts that receive this distinction, and their guests, are honored with a seat at the head table at the Golden Gavel Award Luncheon. The Toastmasters Golden Gavel is the highest award presented by the organization for an individual who demonstrates the utmost level of communication excellence. That year, our governor's wife could not attend and I was invited to sit with him.

The first Golden Gavel was presented in 1959 to Dr. Frank C. Baxter, Professor Emeritus, USC, and television personality. Since then, Golden Gavel recipient list has been graced with several celebrity names including Greer Garson, Walter Cronkite, Dr. Robert Schuler, Dr. Joyce Brothers, Mark Russell, Grace M. Hooper, Zig Ziglar, Debbie Fields Rose (Mrs. Fields) and others. That year, the award went to John W. Warner who would be elected to his first term as U.S. Senator from Virginia in 1978. Seated at the head table, I was privileged to shake hands and chat with the future senator.

Attending the Convention was a delightful experience that I didn't expect to repeat. Little did I know! As it turned out, I attended the International Convention every year until 1990, and I met many very distinguished people. As an added benefit, these gatherings would be set in a new location every year. This, along with my travel for the Center took me to places I would never have visited otherwise.

I only made one FORACS trip that year and that was to St. Croix in the Virgin Islands to train personnel for a new range. I arrived about the time the outer bands of the infamous Hurricane Eloise reached shore. Rain with high winds whipped the area and all Civil Defense and Red Cross personnel were placed on alert. Then the storm moved on and we went about our business, keeping our schedule for the week. I was a little shaken but determined to enjoy my trip.

At that time, St. Croix didn't have the tourist trade that the other islands enjoyed. Still, I found it to be a lovely island. I drove around in my off-work hours and enjoyed the beautiful natural landscape. I visited the places of interest — old sugar mills built in the late 1700s and plantation estates displaying the opulent life-styles of that time. These were my first sightseeing ventures alone.

Soon after John died, I decided that if I wanted to do and see some of the things that interested me, I couldn't sit around and wait for an escort. I had to go alone. I usually took some annual leave whenever I traveled for the Center or to attend Toastmasters events. I rented a car and treated myself to the local sites and places of interest. Making this decision has enriched my life, and once I gained confidence, it led to some interesting experiences.

Often, upon hearing my plans, someone would say to me, "You're not driving alone, are you?"

If they didn't know me very well, I would answer, "Oh no, I usually pick up hitchhikers along the way to keep me company." Then, I'd wait for the gasp!

As lt. governor education, my responsibilities included planning and directing the District 5 Fall Conference. At the planning committee meeting, we chose a county fair theme and made plans that included balloons, clowns and a midway with about 20 booths hosted by areas in the district. When the big day arrived, the convention hall at the Bahia Motor Hotel in Mission Bay Park was filled with creative booths promoting every aspect of Toastmasters. The most popular booth video-taped members and guests as they responded to a Table Topics question. This was a new experience for most of us: video cameras, those huge shoulder-riding monsters that produced VHS and BETA video tapes, had just became available to home-movie enthusiasts. However, those who stayed too long in front of the camera risked missing out on our fabulous door prizes.

Everyone had a card that had to be initialed at every booth in order to be eligible to win a door prize at the banquet. Our door prizes were unique and very desirable—provided by club officials. One officer accompanied the winner on a Saturday morning jog followed by breakfast. Another officer took a pie-in-the-face and one winner received a guided tour of the local community. I offered a gourmet dinner for two at my condo. This was such a hit that I offered the same prize several times in the following years.

We had a record crowd in attendance at the banquet that evening. Notables 2nd Vice President Durwood English, Executive Director Terry McCann and J. Clark Chamberlain mingled with the crowd throughout the day and were duly recognized at the banquet that evening.

Later that evening, as I relaxed in my condo, I knew that everyone had enjoyed the conference. It made the effort worthwhile. I drifted off to sleep with thoughts of my next project whirling in my head.

The winter months arrived in sunny Southern California, and I began laying the groundwork for establishing a new Toastmasters club at the Center's sister facility, the Navy Undersea Center. Starting this new club would fulfill my last requirement in the Toastmasters educational program in order to become a Distinguished Toastmaster, a "DTM."

Chapter 10

HB DTM

I am not sure exactly when I set my sights on DTM certification. Many people who join Toastmasters are satisfied with the personal improvement they gain while working their way through the Communication and Leadership Programs. They maintain their membership until they have reached the desired level of comfort and confidence — then they drop out. Not me. When I reached one goal, another always seemed to catch my eye. Sometime after I learned that only three Toastmasters in all of District 5 had earned the distinction of DTM, I decided I wanted to join that select group.

The Toastmasters educational program has evolved, changing several times over the years. In the early 1970s, there were two manuals with 15 speech projects each. After completing the projects in the first manual, I received a Certificate of Progress and moved on to the second manual. While learning to prepare and deliver these 30 speeches, I overcame my fear of public speaking and discovered that I thoroughly enjoyed "having the lectern." It was just plain fun to say what I intended to say, get my point across, and receive some compliments along with corrective criticism. I listened carefully to each evaluation; my goal was to learn and make each speech better than the last.

When I completed these two manuals, I began working toward Able Toastmaster (ATM) certification which required three years of continuous membership, three speaking engagements outside the Toastmasters organization, plus a term spent serving as a club officer. I fulfilled these requirements, applied for ATM certification, and received my award in September of 1975. By this time — in the course of carrying out my leadership responsibilities — I had fulfilled many of the DTM requirements.

While serving as lt. governor organization in District 5, I conducted a Speechcraft course at the Center. Speechcraft offers an introduction to public speaking and to the Toastmasters experience. The sessions cover a number of topics in the course of four to eight meetings, depending on the length of each meeting, the pace and schedule set by the hosting organization or company. The participants are usually pleased with their improvement and eager to join a Toastmasters club.

In order to boost attendance, I made sure to invite the captain, the Center's commanding officer, to our kick-off session. He attended, and with the draw of his presence, our course was sold out.

The next year, while serving as lt. governor education, I conducted another Toastmasters program at the Center — the Youth Leadership Program. By that time, I had a personal goal in mind; had it not been a DTM requirement, I am certain I would not have tackled this challenging project of working with young people.

About the time I completed my DTM requirements, International President George Scott visited our district. It was the day we were conducting our 45th Annual High School Speech Contest, early in 1976. Since each district can expect a Presidential visit only about once every seven years, I was pleased to have the opportunity to meet our highest official and I was impressed. President Scott was very likeable and approachable. As it turned out, his name would always signify a special event in my life. He signed the charter for Undersea Club No. 888; this signed document fulfilled my last requirement and allowed me to submit my application for DTM certification.

Bob Bolam presenting the Undersea Club Certification - my last DTM requirement.

Courtesy Space and Naval Warfare Systems San Diego

Almost without question, I had met the requirements — except, possibly, for one technicality — I needed my seven months spent as Homer to fulfill the five-year membership requirement. So, after submitting my application, Bob Bolam and I waited anxiously and we wondered, *Would my time before "Helen" count?* Then one day the wait ended: DTM Certificate

No. 365, dated March 15, 1976, and bearing President Scott's signature, arrived.

As Bob made the presentation at the next meeting, he told the club that while over a million people had participated in the Toastmasters program "only 365 such awards have been presented." He went on to say that this particular award was unique — the first earned by a woman. He acknowledged my contribution to Toastmasters, saying, "Helen Blanchard has played a significant part in the integration process of women into Toastmasters. Through her effort, not only has the organization been enhanced but she has accelerated the rate at which women have had made available to them valuable oral communication training."

As Bob placed the certificate in my hands my fellow club members expressed their appreciation for my accomplishment with big smiles and a hearty round of applause.

Shortly thereafter, I ordered personalized license plates for my car and I was quite pleased that California requires plates front and back. Since the day they arrived, "HB DTM" has accompanied me everywhere I have driven and has been relocated four times — cars may change but personalized license plates remain with their owners. My receipt of the DTM prompted an article in the Calendar and the Toastmaster magazine ran a photo of me posing by my car with my license plate clearly in view. I think my father notified the Pender Times so that his friends and neighbors would know that a former Pender girl had made the news in California.

About a month after receiving DTM certification, I was elected District 5 Governor and installed in that office in July.

I was becoming more and more involved with the organization. Though my Toastmasters activities filled my leisure time,

Courtesy Toastmasters International

My "HB DTM" license plates have accompanied me everywhere—cars may change but the license plates remain the same.

including much of my annual leave, they did not take anything away from my dedication to my job at the Center.

I managed Code 6901 and visited the FORACS ranges as needed. My travel for the Center included another visit to AUTEC in the Bahamas, a FORACS range managers meeting in Washington D.C., and a visit to the Applied Physics Laboratory at the University of Washington in Seattle. In recognition of my dedication to my work at the Center, I was nominated for the annual Federal Woman's Award in 1976 and received a Superior Performance Award in January 1977.

By the time I began serving as district governor, the number of women on the Toastmasters roster had steadily increased and other women were climbing the leadership ladder. District 26 in Colorado elected Marilyn Boland governor in 1975 and she holds the distinction of being the first woman to serve in this office. The following year, I was elected governor in District 5 and Doreen Henley was elected in District 60, in Canada.

The District 5 installation banquet was a formal affair held at the Atlantis Restaurant near San Diego Sea World and Mission Bay. During the ceremony, the outgoing officers were recognized and dismissed with words of appreciation and the new officers were installed by the installation officer, Bob Bolam.

J. Clarke Chamberlain and his wife attended, and the outgoing district governor had the honor of presenting J. Clark with the Communication and Leadership Award. This is a prestigious award given in recognition of a significant contribution to community affairs. J. Clark was certainly an ideal recipient with a long list of service including: chairman of the Community Christmas Center Committee in charge of decorations at San Diego's Balboa Park, member of the American Society of Association Executives, a director of the Better Business Bureau, 1st vice president of Goodwill Industries, a member of the Rotary and the San Diego Chamber of Commerce.

Cheryl and Bruce were there to see me installed as district governor but I was escorted by Douglas McHugh, the incoming district secretary. In the next few years, Doug and I enjoyed a close friendship. He shared my enthusiasm for the program, escorted me to many Toastmasters events, and helped Bob in my campaigns for international director.

I traveled to the International Convention in New Orleans a few weeks after being installed as governor. During the Convention, all the district governors were invited to a special breakfast to hear the new International President speak. Doreen and I were the only women in the audience — and possibly the first women to attend such an event. The meeting began with an invocation which ended with the words, "... and at the end of our terms, may we be better men for having served as district governors." Before the "amen" my eyes popped open and met Doreen's. We never did determine if those words were spoken out of habit or if this was done deliberately.

As had become my routine by that time, I took a few days extra leave to tour New Orleans and thoroughly enjoyed the sights and atmosphere of the old Southern city. Upon returning to San Diego, I tackled the usual flurry of Toastmasters activity the autumn months bring. I attended area speech contests, our district conference, and made an appearance at several other district conferences in Region II, including Founders District Conference in Claremont and District 52 Conference in Burbank. Toastmasters President Robert Blakeley spoke at the District 52 Conference. He chose "Be Proud You're a Toastmaster" as the theme for his presidency and this was the topic of his speech. Although I don't remember his exact words I

Blanchard Collection

District 5 officers installed in July 1976. (Left to right) Dennis Lake, organizational lt. governor; Douglas McHugh, district secretary; Larry Mulvey, administrative lt. governor; Helen Blanchard, district governor; N.S. Bernard, educational lt. governor; Al Meloche, district treasurer. We were a hard-working, compatible group and enjoyed a busy and rewarding year.

still remember the essence of his inspiring speech and how it related to me and my personal pride in being a Toastmaster.

Since I took office in July, the end of the year marked the midway point in my term. January arrived with a continuation of my responsibilities as governor: the usual club visits, installing officers, presenting charters, and presenting certificates to Youth Leadership and Speechcraft graduates. Looking back over my notes for the year I discovered that the horoscope Taurus predicted that people born under this sign would be given more responsibility with more pressure, but if they stood tall and steady the rewards could be considerable. Of course, the accuracy of this prediction would not be determined for a while.

One of my Toastmasters visits took me to Baja California and the Presidential Fronterizo Club, in Mexico. Jerry Garcia, a member of that club, handed me a note written in Spanish accompanied by the English translation. It read, "I wish the best and precious life for you and I believe that some day you will be World President."

I assumed that he meant Toastmasters International President. "World" President? *A woman?* This was the first time I heard mention of such a thing and I laughed...at first. But, the seed was planted. I don't think there was an actual day or time when I began to think of the Toastmasters Presidency as a definite goal. It came about gradually and in the natural progression of leadership positions. However, I remember attending a seminar in November, 1978, where I was asked to make a list of long term goals. Toastmasters President made the list but nowhere near the top; good health and professional speaker occupied the first two slots.

I was dedicated to the organization and completely convinced that Toastmasters training is of tremendous value to people in almost all walks of life — everyone needs to communicate effectively! I was always on the lookout for ways to make these benefits known and to promote Toastmasters.

One day, while reading Mel Thompson's syndicated column, "Working it Out" in the *San Diego Union-Tribune*, I saw an opportunity. In this column, Mel answered a question about sources of help for people who have trouble expressing themselves. He recommended joining a community theater group but missed offering the best suggestion. Oh, my! I had some information he would welcome! I invited him to a Toastmasters meeting, he attended, and after that he became a dedicated advocate of Toastmasters International.

Later, after I became an International Director, Mel opened doors for me to spread the word about Toastmasters through TV and radio appearances. Meanwhile, as I neared the completion of my term as district governor (the highest office in the district), other doors were beginning to open, and the first-level international office seemed to beckon to me.

I had become a very visible member of the district leadership, recognized and well-received at the International Convention as District 5 Governor. With encouragement from those who knew me best throughout District 5 and Region II (plus a nod from Bob), I began thinking about moving to the international arena. In fact, I decided to throw my hat in the ring. Toastmasters' top leadership consists of a Board of International Directors led by an International President. I set my sights on becoming one of the directors.

Campaigning for International Director is far reaching and backing at the district and regional level including financial support for the expensive campaign was essential. Once the news that I was considering a run for international office began to spread, the response was very encouraging. Several supporters offered to host fund-raising parties in support of my candidacy. In June, the election process of the international directors begins at the regional conference.

The regional conference always is a purpose-driven event with a fully-packed morning-to-night schedule. On Friday and Saturday, a member of the Executive Committee and the two International Directors from the region plus a staff member from Toastmasters World Headquarters (WHQ) conduct a two-day training session for the newly-elected officers from each district. Besides this training session for lt. governors and governors, a speech contest is held to select a contestant for the

International Speech Contest and the International Director candidates are elected.

The event draws many Toastmasters who are not training, campaigning, or competing for a spot in the international speech competition—and they enjoy a full schedule. On Friday, humorous speeches take the spotlight in an entertaining *theme night* that often calls for costumes. Saturday morning is set aside for educational and motivational speakers followed by a luncheon with a business meeting and the International Director election that afternoon. A formal banquet on Saturday night marks the end of the conference.

That year, our regional conference was held at the Sheraton Universal Hotel in North Hollywood. As a special treat, Hollywood celebrity George Jessell delivered the keynote speech at the luncheon. It's an amusing coincidence that President Franklin D. Roosevelt had once named Mr. Jessell "Toastmaster General of the United States" in recognition of his delivery of more than 300 after-dinner speeches.

Following this outstanding and very entertaining speaker, each of the three candidates for International Director was given eight minutes to present his or her qualifications, take questions from the floor, or divide the time between these two alternatives. I chose the third alternative. In closing my talk, I stated that I was a widow; my children were grown so I could devote all my nonworking time to the Toastmasters program and followed with, "Are there any questions?"

The very first question posed by an elderly man stopped the clock and hushed the crowd. "What happens if you get pregnant?" he asked.

I froze in a room of absolute silence.

What was he calling me?

Table Topics had never prepared me for a mean-spirited question like this. Every response that came to mind failed to be appropriate for a potential International Director. Finally, after what seemed like an eternity, I responded with, "Let's limit this to questions about Toastmasters, please. May I have the next question?" I actually heard the audience start breathing again! After the luncheon, several people complimented me on the way I had handled that awkward situation.

The election took place on the afternoon of June 3rd. According to Toastmasters election rules, if one candidate garners 75 percent of the vote, that person goes to the International Convention as the International Director candidate from the region. This is not likely on the first ballot if there are three or more candidates. For a crowded ballot, there is a run-off election between the two candidates with the highest number of votes.

As it turned out, there were initially three candidates running in our region. After the first ballot, I found myself one of the top two, but I was facing competition from John Latin, a member of the larger Founder's District. The second ballot gave John 58 percent of the vote and 42 percent went to me. Since neither of us received 75 percent we would both move ahead to the competition at the International Convention in Toronto, Canada.

Immediately, we kicked off the second phase of my campaign with over 50 supporters attending a fund-raising party. This was followed a month later with another big party. Cards from well-wishers began arriving in my mailbox; some contained donations. Once the money began to flow I gladly accepted Past District Governor Dick Freedman's offer to serve as my campaign treasurer. District 5 fully supported my candidacy and during visits to other districts throughout the region, I received promises of support.

In the weeks between the regional conference in June and the August International Convention, my life went on. I made a trip to AUTEC in the Bahamas with a stop in the Midwest to visit relatives. Along with those two big fund-raising parties for my Toronto-bound campaign, I was kept very busy.

About a dozen District 5 supporters traveled from San Diego to Toronto for the International Conference that August and two very supportive people from the Data Bank came along as well. Proud of the fact that we were an international district with clubs in Baja, Mexico, we all wore brightly colored Mexican boleros. We also served margaritas, a popular Mexican drink, in our hospitality room. Of course, we offered non-alcoholic beverages, as well.

My campaign workers and I spent hours on the floor. We handed out my brochure and talked to as many voters as possible. I learned to look for carpeted areas to ease the pain of standing in high heels while I greeted people, shook hands and smiled. I didn't wear Vaseline on my teeth — as I had heard some models do — though maybe I should have. I didn't notice until it was over but all that smiling was very tiring. Our campaign seemed be going well, I heard encouraging comments, and I thought I might win.

When the votes were counted, Durwood English was elected International President and John Latin was the new International Director from Region II.

I lost.

Until this time, I had worked very hard in some campaigns with stiff competition. I had also experienced some discouraging events along the way, but I had always finished as a winner. This loss hit me hard. I felt I had let so many people down: those people who traveled to Toronto to support me and the others back in San Diego who cheered me on and donated to my campaign. Negative thoughts began to run through my mind that evening. *Am I going too fast? Maybe the organization just isn't ready for a woman in an international office? Is there something about me that people don't like?* I shed a few tears that evening. However, I had to pull myself together to make an appearance at the Convention the next day. A photo was taken of me accepting the Distinguished District Certificate earned by District 5 under my governorship. A close inspection of the photo reveals that my eyes were still a little swollen.

I don't talk much about this defeat in my speeches except to tell the story of one kindly older Toastmaster gentleman who took me aside afterward and told me that this was probably good for me. "Separates the men from the boys," he said. Bless him. He was serious as he passed this wisdom on to me and apparently completely unaware that this cliché did not quite apply.

On my way back to San Diego from Toronto, I changed planes in Chicago and called my brother Milt who still lived in Waukegan. I told him the outcome of the election with unconcealed disappointment in my voice.

Of course, he made an attempt to cheer me up — "Hey, Sis," he said. "Don't take it so hard. You know, you're doing really well for a woman!"

Let's just say that Milt's attempt at lifting my spirits that August in 1977 failed. However, later, at the appropriate time, this story would elicit laughter from over 1000 people, including Milt.

Supporters greeted me when I arrived in San Diego, and in the next few days I received several encouraging calls from outside District 5. Knowing that others shared my disappointment made it easier to bear and before long I was ready to immerse myself in Toastmasters again.

I had experienced victory and defeat; I had more responsibility and more pressure at the Center and in Toastmasters. But the rewards, indeed, had been "considerable." Thus, the horoscope predictions for Taurus seemed to ring true.

Chapter 11

Moving On Up

When I returned from Toronto, I was a "Toastmaster without an office" for the first time since I'd been installed as treasurer of the Center's club in January, 1971. Over the years, serving in Toastmasters had become a way of life for me and I wanted an active role in the organization — one in which I could make a difference. As I began investigating the possibilities, I found that the new district governor had not yet found a new club chairman. Such a role seemed perfect for this time in my Toastmasters career — so I volunteered. As it turned out, starting new clubs was a demanding and time-consuming task. But it confirmed for me that introducing people to the Toastmasters program opened doors for them and changed lives — I enjoyed it immensely.

WHQ offered a brief directive on forming new clubs that I found helpful. However, I was on my own in areas the directive didn't cover, and once I chose a prospective location, I did whatever it took to establish the new club and make it a success. On one occasion, I donned a hardhat and walked through the shipyard to a meeting room at the National Steel and Shipbuilding Company (NASSCO) in San Diego. I thought this was pretty special until a friend sent me a newspaper clipping that mentioned a Toastmasters meeting at the Treehouse Fun Ranch, a nudist colony in Devore, California. I wonder how they conducted the demonstration meeting for that club!

The first club chartered in 1978 was at the Naval Station on 32nd Street. We had a good turnout from the beginning, and the 20 members needed to charter the club were on the roster within a few weeks. Most of our new clubs, however, weren't established this easily. Another location, which became The Toastmasters of La Jolla, proved to be far more difficult to form and charter. We advertised again and again, met week after week, and asked those who came to bring a friend to the next meeting. It took 20 meetings to sign up the necessary 20 members. I have to credit the determination of Dr. Carson Lewis, a prominent physician in La Jolla, for his role in chartering this club. Today, while some of my clubs — such as the one at the Naval Station — have faded into the past, Toastmasters of La Jolla is a dynamic group of multinational professionals boasting a large membership.

There were 53 clubs in the District when I took office and 62 at the end of my term. With nine new clubs, my new club committee set a record for District 5 that year. After this experience, I had a good idea of what worked and what didn't. So, I wrote some guidelines that included ideas for finding suitable new club locations, a sample news release, recommendations for mentoring a new club, etc. I created a cover page, made copies of my guidelines plus the WHQ directive, and stapled all nine pages together to produce a small booklet titled, New Club Ideas. I made my booklet available to anyone who wanted it.

All this time, I had been thinking about the coming international election. I'd completed my term as new club chairman and was ready to move ahead. Bob's urging, along with dozens of supportive letters and calls, gave me the needed boost and my hat flew into the ring for a second run at becoming International Director.

On the campaign trail again, I kept a heavy schedule visiting as many Region II districts as possible before the Regional Convention in June. One weekend, I campaigned in Monterey (in the San Francisco area) and Fullerton (near Los Angeles) on the same day. I couldn't have made the trip between the two conferences without the generosity of one of my opponents. Pete Kittredge, who piloted a private plane, planned the trip to campaign on his own behalf and invited me to ride along. This kind of comradeship between Toastmasters candidates vying for the same office made campaigning a pleasant experience. We each worked hard, trying to win votes based on our own merit. There was no bitterness, and no tactics were used to undermine the voters' perception of the character of any other Toastmaster.

At the Region II Conference in Claremont, California, that year, a dedicated group from District 5, including Bob Bolam and Doug McHugh, mingled with the crowd and worked the floor to gain votes for me. Even though there were four candidates in the race, we hoped to receive 75 percent of the vote — the magic number that takes a regional candidate to the International Convention unopposed. I had such strong support going in that we thought this just might happen — and it almost did! When the vote was tallied, I had 70 percent of the vote while my three opponents each garnered a share of the remaining 30 percent. In the final count, Bill Vedier, from District 49 (Hawaii), was the runner-up and the

**Dedication and Service
to
Districts
in
Region II**

HELEN BLANCHARD, DTM

HELEN ATTENDED THE FOLLOWING DURING 1977/78

March 12, 1977	Governor's Conference, San Francisco
April 30, 1977	District 33 Conference, Bakersfield (Educational Speaker)
May 21, 1977	District One Conference, Culver City (Educational Speaker)
June 11, 1977	District Four Executive Meeting, San Jose
June 17-18, 1977	Region II Conference, Universal City (Educational Speaker)
July 8, 1977	District One Installation
August 17-20, 1977	International Conference, Toronto
September 10, 1977	Governors Conference, Fullerton
October 22, 1977	District One Conference, Los Angeles (Educational Speaker)
November 5, 1977	District Four Conference, Santa Clara (Educational Speaker)
November 19, 1977	District 52 Conference, Burbank (Educational Speaker)
November 19, 1977	Founders District Conference, Palm Springs (Educational Speaker)
February 17, 1978	International Board Meeting, Santa Ana
March 11, 1978	Governors Conference, Burbank
May 5, 1978	District One Conference, Los Angeles
May 6, 1978	District 33 Conference, China Lake
May 13, 1978	District 52 Conference, Van Nuys (Educational Speaker)
May 20, 1978	District Four Conference, Monterey (Educational Speaker)
May 20, 1978	Founders District Conference, Fullerton (Educational Speaker)

Vote for Helen Blanchard, DTM

The Best Qualified Candidate

Blanchard Collection

This campaign flier shows my heavy schedule for Region II visits while running for International Director in 1977 and 1978.

two of us had about two months to prepare our campaigns for the International Convention in Vancouver.

As they had done the year before, several of my supporters hosted fund-raising parties throughout the month of July
to help finance my second campaign. The parties promised
a stimulating evening with entertainment designed to at-
tract a crowd. Of course, some of our finest speakers were on
hand with humorous speeches. The best entertainment was a
display of hidden talent — three of our staid past district governors stole the show when they emerged from the crowd in
elaborate, exotic costumes and performed their rendition of
The Dance of the Seven Veils.

By the middle of August, I was ready for the campaign in
Vancouver. I had written letters to the district governors inviting them to visit my hospitality room and pick up a copy of
New Club Ideas. Most of them did, so we entertained a steady
flow of guests. I appreciated the help of volunteers from District 5 who kept the finger-food platters piled high and our
visitors glasses filled.

On Thursday, the conference schedule included the International Business Meeting in the morning followed by the election. This was a high-tension day. The old thoughts whirled in
my head: *Was it too soon for a woman? Was I about to face another
devastating defeat? What then?* As the candidates were presented, I was surprised to find that I faced two opponents instead
of the one, as expected. My pilot friend, Pete Kittredge "ran
from the floor" and received five percent of the vote while Bill
Vedier received nine percent — leaving 4715 votes, representing
86 percent of the international vote, for me — a landslide! My
fears that the Toastmasters of the world were not ready for a
woman in an international office vanished.

Looking back, I am grateful that I didn't receive that coveted
75 percent of the vote at the regional conference. If I had, I

would not have had the assurance that Toastmasters outside our region would accept me when I served my two year term as International Director.

The Convention came to a close after the President's Dinner Dance that evening. During this event, outgoing International President Durwood English passed the Presidential mantle to Hurbert (Dobbie) Dobson, and the outgoing directors pinned their newly-elected successors.

As Vit Eckersdorf from District 4 (the San Francisco area) removed the pin from his lapel and placed it at the neckline of my dress he said, "Helen, I am proud and pleased that you will be wearing the same pin I have worn." Vit had been an excellent director, liked and respected by all who knew him, and I was proud to receive the pin he had worn.

At that time, there were 16 Directors, two from each of the eight North American regions. Since then, the by-laws have been changed to allow two directors representing districts from other continents. The term of office is two years, so half the directors — one from each region — is elected each year. Each director serves on a committee and I was assigned to the District Administration and Programming Committee.

After I returned to San Diego, I invited Toastmasters and friends to an open house to celebrate my victory. About 50 people made their way to my condo patio to offer congratulations and celebrate with good food, drink, and warm conversation. In the following days, my mailbox almost overflowed with cards and letters of congratulations. WHQ issued a press release; numerous newspapers picked up the story and my name made the headlines in newspaper business sections across the nation. This was a heady time for the Toastmasters portion of my life.

As a newly elected member of the International Board of Directors in 1978, I chose my outfit to blend in with the tuxedos. The other Board members included,

Seated, left to right: Terry McCann (Executive Director), Durwood English (Immediate Past President), Bill Hamilton (3rd VP), Hubert "Dobby" Dobson (President), Eric Stuhlmueller (Senior VP), Pat Panfile (2nd VP), Herbert Wellner (Secretary/Treasurer)
Second Row: All International Directors - Larry Selby, Ted Wilga, Hubert "Butch" Barney, John Latin, Helen Blanchard, Bill Crawford, Eddie Dunn, Nath Nayak
Top Row: All International Directors - Sid Smith, Fritz Schroedor, Oscar Olive, Carl Johnson, Neil Wilkenson, Floyd Swathwood, Bill Miller

Meanwhile, my work at the Center took on an international flavor, as well. NATO FORACS became a reality and a new range was about to become operational with a newly-hired group of engineers ready for training in FORACS data processing. Just six days after returning from Vancouver, I boarded a plane headed for Stavanger, Norway. The NATO range, located at Stavanger on the shores of the North Sea, had been under construction for the previous two years and was now ready for operation. I witnessed the ribbon cutting ceremony that signified transferring command of the range to the Norwegian Navy under the guidance of Captain Tor Berg, the new range manager. The first ships to be tested were the frigate HMS Arrow, flying the U.K. flag, and Theseus, a German ship. Although I was aboard both vessels during the dockside portion of the test, I spent most of my time in the engineering office and computer room. Since I needed to oversee the data processing from data gathering to the final report, I stayed in Norway for four weeks, longer than any of the others in the San Diego group.

We were quartered on the Norwegian base in a barracks-type building. My room included private toilet facilities, but we all shared a common shower. When it was my turn, I posted a sign on the door to assure my privacy, reading: STAY OUT—HELEN IS HERE.

As it turned out, most of the Norwegian Navy personnel took leave in August including the kitchen staff. Fortunately, Captain Berg's wife, Katrina, rode her bicycle to the barracks and prepared a hearty Norwegian breakfast for us. At noon, we had cold cuts for sandwiches and we drove into the city for dinner each evening. The whole team enjoyed Norwegian hospitality, but I was especially appreciative of the Berg's effort. As usual, I was the only woman on the training team, and this was an extra long stay. Throughout that month, Katrina and Tor Berg made a special effort to help me feel more comfortable. We became good friends, and I later had the good fortune to visit with them again.

I enjoyed working with the engineers as I took them through the steps of FORACS data processing: collection, analysis and report preparation. Although English was their second language, we communicated well, and by the time I left, they were ready to take over the operation on their own. In recognition of this achievement, the entire training crew received a letter of commendation from the NATO FORACS Steering Committee after the range was certified.

As had become my custom, I took advantage of my leisure time to explore the local area. Stavanger, located at the gateway to Fjord Country, is a fascinating Scandinavian city. I was impressed with the mix of old and new.

The remains of the old fishing village hugged the waterfront while nearby modern office buildings housed international companies and late-model cars dominated the traffic in the streets. One weekend, a group of us ventured into the countryside, making stops at an Iron Age farm and some ancient cemeteries.

On my last weekend in Norway, I decided to venture into the country north of Stavanger on my own. I was assured that traveling alone would be safe, so, with map in hand and a sense of adventure, I boarded a bus headed north. Following my preplanned route, I transferred from bus to ferry, then back to bus for a ride to the next ferry landing.

As I traveled further and further from Stavanger, I noticed that I was hearing less and less English. Then there was none. The language barrier made me very uneasy, especially since I didn't know what to expect from the darkening sky. When heavy rain began to fall, I decided to retrace my route back to Stavanger. Although I was disappointed that I failed to reach my destination, I had chalked up a great travel adventure to keep forever in my memories.

Stavanger was the principal city of Norway's oil industry, and two state-owned oil companies were located there. The employees of these companies made up the membership of Norway's only Toastmaster's club. I had contacted the club before I left San Diego and received an invitation to be a guest speaker at their September meeting.

As an International Director, I was pleased to have the opportunity to visit the Toastmasters club in this Scandinavian country.

I returned to sunny San Diego before the harsh Norwegian winter arrived. Back at the Center, my responsibilities increased; each range FORACS added meant more data to add to the summary reports. In addition to providing quality control for data analysis and technical writing, I monitored a major contract for software development. This included rewriting software for range testing and analysis plus creating software to run new computer hardware for the NATO FORACS office in Brussels, Belgium.

In addition to my Data Bank and FORACS responsibilities, as a division head, I was involved with areas of general management practices at the Center. By the mid-70s Equal Employment Opportunity measures were in place and EEO was a buzzword that caused management heads to turn. The Center enacted a program called "Upward Mobility" that was designed within the Federal Service to "provide the maximum feasible opportunity to employees to enhance their skills." Translating this Federal jargon into everyday language: this was an opportunity for managers to look for people in dead-end jobs and offer them a new position and training that would lead to a career with better advancement possibilities. We were always looking for someone, usually a secretary, to offer Upward Mobility.

One day, after I had looked through a stack of applications, my supervisor asked me if I had found a candidate for the program.

"I have good news and bad news." I paused and smiled. "I found an excellent candidate. The bad news is, she's your secretary."

He, of course, was glad to give her this opportunity and she was one of the three I moved into the program over a period of time.

While my job and Toastmasters kept me busy, I reserved some time for family and friends. That year, I visited Cheryl and her new husband in Simi Valley, California, made a trip to the Midwest to attend my nephew's wedding, and spent a few days at Thanksgiving in Nebraska with Dad and Irene. On the social side, I invited friends and Data Bank crew to watch the annual Parade of Lights from my condo. At that time, the parade route for this spectacular Christmas display of decorated boats stretched across San Diego Bay from the tip of Shelter Island to Coronado. Carrying on John's tradition — Blanchard's Blast every summer in Allied Gardens, the Parade of Lights Party at Helen's condo became a yearly event, as well.

In any circle of friends and colleagues, sad times come, and the Toastmasters circle is no different. I was saddened when I heard the news that J. Clark Chamberlain had passed away on December 21, 1978. Reaching the age of 83, he had lived a full life, much of it dedicated to Toastmasters and the San Diego community. Still, we mourned the loss of this fine gentleman and

Toastmasters pioneer. A few months later, my good friend, Doug McHugh died suddenly of a heart attack at the young age of 45.

And then, loss struck my own family. In the fall, a fatal stroke took Dad from us. In his 92 years, he touched many lives and was so loved in the community. Just about everyone in Pender attended his funeral.

Although this period of my life was marked with sadness, such is the way of things. We enjoy the good times and grieve when sadness comes — all the while, acquiring memories to savor later.

Midway through my first year as International Director, Durwood English and I launched a club for advanced speakers. This club was a new concept that attracted Toastmasters who had earned ATM or DTM certification and needed evaluation on 20 to 30 minute speeches. Some of these Toastmasters were aspiring professional speakers. We named the new club, Excelsior, and it continues to thrive today.

Late in January, I received the agenda that would be presented at the February Board Meeting. I studied the material and prepared myself to participate. Since I was the first woman to serve on the Toastmasters International Board of Directors, I wanted to meld into the distinguished group without particular notice. The other Board members, however, wanted to make me feel welcome. The first day of the meeting was on Valentines Day, and as I took my seat I noticed a lovely red rose next to my name plate. Although I recognized President Dobby Dobson's thoughtfulness in choosing to honor me this way, I felt odd, singled out, and different.

I felt even more uncomfortable when the legal consul, Joe Rinnert — who spoke at every Board Meeting — began with,

"Gentlemen," followed by a long, deliberate pause before adding, "…and lady." For those who have known Joe, you can imagine the sparkle in his eye when he did so. Once he realized that I was uncomfortable, he changed his opening to "Members of the Board." I didn't want special recognition as a woman; I just wanted to be one of the directors.

As International Director, I took on a more visible role in Toastmasters, the Center and the community. I joined the National Speakers Association (NSA), an organization founded by Toastmaster Cavett Robert in 1973. The NSA is dedicated to advancing the art and value of professional speakers. I met many talented professional speakers in this organization and also expanded my opportunities for speaking engagements while entering a new arena for my own professionalism — radio and television appearances.

As I mentioned earlier, Mel Thompson (a San Diego based syndicated newspaper columnist) became a Toastmasters advocate and opened media doors for me. As a result of his influence and recommendation, I presented a series of five talks on communication on KSDO radio over a six month period. Mel also arranged appearances on two popular local television programs.

The first was *Sun-Up*, local competition for the popular national morning shows, *Good Morning America* and the *Today Show*. The second was *The International Hour*, which focused on local people involved in international affairs in some way. These opportunities to talk about the Toastmasters program were fun and a new way for me to promote the organization.

Mel's community service and support of the Toastmasters program did not go unnoticed. At our district installation banquet that year, he was presented with our Communication and Leadership Award along with a hearty "thank you" for spreading the word about our program in his syndicated columns and in his career management business.

The Center noticed that I was moving up the rungs of the Toastmasters leadership ladder. To them, this indicated additional expertise and qualifications. Command asked me to develop a "Better Briefing" workshop for higher-level personnel who often made briefings to the Center's sponsors in Washington D.C. My schedule was already overloaded but this task really appealed to me. Perhaps the school teacher urge kicked in, prompting me to respond with a definite "Yes" to a project that was to be developed in my spare time — after work and between Toastmasters commitments. Thus, the many hours that went into the preparation of this three-day seminar were spread over several months.

About the same time, the Equal Employment Opportunity Office (EEO) asked me to give a series of lunchtime presentations on communication.

I conducted these "Brown Bag Lunches" at two locations within the Center: Topside (the facility on the hill) and Bayside (on the shoreline).

I continued to make Toastmasters better known at the Center, and my work received recognition from upper management. I couldn't predict that, one day in the future, my after-hours work and Toastmasters experience would actually save my career.

In the fall, I received my first request to speak professionally — for a fee. I traveled to Disneyland in Anaheim to speak at a meeting of the Women's Council of Realtors. I decided to donate the money I received to the Ralph Smedley Memorial

Fund. If it weren't for Smedley's concept of the Toastmasters program — and all the valuable training I had received as a result — I certainly wouldn't have had this opportunity.

I've always been thankful for Dr. Smedley's generosity. He could have made a fortune from his idea for helping young men overcome their fear of public speaking. He chose, instead, to create a nonprofit, non-commercial movement. He replied to those who criticized this decision that he "would rather be rich in friendship than money." He has touched the life of everyone who has benefited from the Toastmasters program. If these are considered friends, then Dr. Smedley's circle of friends has exceeded 4 million and continues to grow. By his standard, he is indeed rich, and his idea has made many others rich, as well.

Chapter 12

The Big Decision

In January of 1980, I stood before an audience of 250 Rotarians and Rotary Anns in Escondido, California, to deliver a motivational speech about choices that influence one's future. Thanks to Toastmasters training, I felt at home at the lectern and completely at ease as I gazed out over this audience of strangers, many of whom were highly-educated professionals. They gave me their undivided attention from the beginning of my talk to the end, then burst into applause as they rose to their feet. This was my first standing ovation from a non-Toastmasters audience. What a thrill!

Before I had the benefit of Toastmasters training, I could barely muster the courage to stand before a small group of FORACS range personnel to make the training presentation my job required. But that was in the past. By this time, presentations associated with my job came easy, I was conducting communication workshops and seminars, and my schedule was peppered with speaking engagements.

That spring, as International Director, I was a featured speaker at Toastmasters conferences in Honolulu, San Jose, Buena Park and San Diego. Many of my speeches were focused on communication and leadership. Most fit into a motivational, educational, informative or inspirational category, and I drew material for these talks from life experiences. My brother Earle's accident, recovery and business success provided personal experience material for many of my positive attitude speeches. I enjoyed talking about my school teaching days, and later, my granddaughters provided humorous incidents I could share with pride. Over the years, I have given hundreds of speeches and thousands of people probably feel they know my family personally (especially those two granddaughters who brought me so much joy as children and continue to do so as young women).

Many of the people who knew me from Toastmasters arranged for me to speak to other organizations. Of course, there were now a good number of women members who wanted to spread the Toastmasters story to women's groups. On one occasion, I conducted a mini-seminar about the Toastmasters program to the Women's Caucus at the University of California at San Diego. About that same time, I presented a communication seminar to the Society of Women Engineers. I was always delighted to be able to reach out to women. Although I have never been an activist in the women's movement and do not approve of the aggressive tactics some of the women's organizations have used; I have always been supportive of equal opportunity, equal pay and equal training. I welcomed the opportunity to encourage women and motivate them toward Toastmasters training. Many women, after hearing my talk, admitted to me that they had not thought about becoming "women on the move." They hadn't realized that learning to "present with confidence" could boost their careers.

When the invitation to the San Diego No. 7 reunion arrived in April of 1980, the absence of the handwritten note at the bottom reminded me that J. Clark was gone; he would miss the club's 50th anniversary celebration. However, members of No. 7 carried on the tradition of welcoming me to this all-male club's event, as J. Clark had done since the second year I served as a district officer. I continued to be an invited guest until 1986. After I became President, they made me an honorary member and contributed to the Ralph Smedley Fund in my name. The Club No. 7 president who bestowed the honor assured everyone that, "J. Clark would heartily approve."

It was standard procedure that—as an International Director—I would oversee the regional conference in my home region during the second year of my term. That year, Region II's conference was held in Culver City, California, and was hosted by District 1. I worked closely with the host district chairman, Ken Himes, who did an outstanding job of making this event a spectacular success. Our honored guests included the top brass of Toastmasters International: International President, 2nd Vice President and Executive Director—posts filled by Durwood English, William Hamilton, and Terry McCann.

As usual, the conference was a mixture of entertainment and education. We kicked off the entertainment portion with a nautical theme night which called for pirate and naval costumes.

A roast headlined the program that evening and it is possible that I was the first woman ever to be roasted at a Toastmasters regional conference. The ten-year shared experiences of Homer and Helen provided a vast amount of material the roasters used to rock the room with laughter. I enjoyed every minute of this hilarious evening.

On Nautical Theme Night at the Region II Conference in Culver City, California, I presented a plaque of appreciation to Ken Himes for his work as Host Chairman.

Besides being the victim for the roast — managing speaker arrangements and keeping the sessions on schedule were my chief responsibilities. I had invited Carol Sapin Gold to speak at the luncheon. She was (and still is) considered an authority on business relations and many Fortune 500 companies have used her consulting services for years. I had attended her management Seminar for Career Women and benefited from her message. I was certain she would be a big hit at the conference, and I was eager for the attendees to benefit from her expertise.

All was going well until lunchtime arrived. Two of our three morning sessions ended on time. The third was dragging on past its allotted limit. Meanwhile, everyone's luncheon salads were on the tables and beginning to wilt, Carol was waiting to be introduced, and this third presenter continued to drone on. I must confess that I've always been a purist as far as time is concerned, and this behavior was testing my patience. From the back of the room, I tried to get his attention with all sorts of non-verbal motions commonly used to tell a speaker to "wrap it up."

He was on a roll — encouraging everyone to express their feelings to the people they loved. "Tell them," he kept repeating, adding, "Hug them and kiss them before it is too late." He went on and on.

Terry McCann was standing next to me. "What should I do?" I asked in desperation.

"You're in charge. You're the International Director."

I didn't want to embarrass the speaker so I couldn't use the old shepherd's crook to drag him to the sidelines. Then, on impulse and completely out of character, I acted on what he was saying. I tore down the aisle shouting, "I love you, too; kiss me!" Then I threw my arms around him, pulled his ear close, and whispered, "Quit. Right now!" An expression of shock crossed his face as he pivoted toward the audience blurting, "So in conclusion..."

This conference was my last big responsibility as International Director. I truly thought this position would be the zenith of my Toastmasters career and frequently referred to this event as my "swan song." On the last evening, as I walked into the elegantly decorated banquet hall, I realized that Ken Himes had incorporated my comment into the banquet theme and placed a lovely ceramic swan in the centerpiece on each table. It was, indeed, a memorable occasion for me. However, it was not my swan song. And as things turned out — it was only a prelude to the zenith of my Toastmasters career.

August arrived too soon and I was on my way to Milwaukee, Wisconsin, and the International Convention. The preceding two years had been rewarding and filled with memorable experiences. At the President's Dinner Dance, as I passed my International Director pin to my successor, Ray Brooks, I knew he would do a good job, but I was so sad that my term had come to an end. That night, along with the other out-going directors, I received a plaque thanking Helen M. Blanchard for "his" service as International Director. I smiled to myself; my goal had been to become just another member of the Board. Obviously, I had done it! And, a short time later I did receive a corrected plaque.

Over the years, I had accumulated a number of Toastmasters lapel pins in recognition of my service and achievements. They are all of a similar design based on the Toastmasters insignia with an inscription that identifies a specific office or award. After each election, the out-going international officers pass their pins to their successors in a pinning ceremony. Each outgoing officer then receives a "past" pin for the office served. A small diamond accent distinguishes the International President and past president pins. Toastmasters at all levels wear their pins with pride. I wear my current pin everywhere I go. When someone notices, I take the opportunity to tell him or her about Toastmasters. I have done this since the day I received my membership pin.

And so, on that night I couldn't help but look around at the lapels of my fellow Toastmasters. I'd enjoyed participating at the international level, and I knew I wanted to continue the climb. By the end of the evening, I had my eye on the Toastmasters International pin that bears that small diamond.

Before attaining higher office could become my goal, I had to consider the other aspects of my life. This new endeavor would be time consuming and demanding, requiring dedication and determination beyond anything in my previous Toastmasters experience. Could I do this without jeopardizing my career at the Center? That job paid the bills and provided health insurance and my retirement plan. By this time, I had an accumulation of strong evidence that my Toastmasters activities did not interfere with my job performance.

In fact, it seemed to enhance it. The Brown Bag Luncheons, Better Briefing Workshops and Speechcraft Youth Leadership training for the summer aids — my Toastmasters experience made these events possible and they all benefited the Center. Over the years, I had received several awards and recognition from the Center and my Toastmasters activities were often mentioned in the justification for the award. That summer, I received notice that I was being considered for the Center's Outstanding Supervisor of the Year award. About that same time, I received a Superior Achievement Award. It was obvious that my superiors recognized my Toastmasters training and that it was an asset to my career.

At this point, the FORACS ranges were all operational with fully-trained personnel. My travel duties for the Center were minimal. I only made one business trip that year — a visit to Range V located on St. Croix in the Virgin Islands. I had acquired a very efficient staff and my branch operated smoothly.

We welcomed some excitement and change in our regular routine that year as we took on a new venture: a video production about FORACS. The presentation covered the entire testing process including the Data Bank. My office was too small to accommodate the camera crew so we taped my segment in a large office that belonged to the head of the Technical Information Division. It occupied a second floor corner in a building located on the crest of Point Loma (prime real estate that belongs to the Navy). The panorama from the window included the Pacific Ocean on one side and San Diego Bay on the other. It was a wonderful backdrop for the FORACS video

and I was delighted to narrate my segment sitting at the desk
in this impressive office. All was well with my world.

Once I made my decision to run for 3rd International Vice
President, I couldn't just leap into my campaign. There was
protocol to follow and, as it turned out, the outcome of the
election at the International Convention in Milwaukee put
me on hold for a year. John Latin, from Founders District in
Region II, lost his bid for 3rd Vice President that summer and
it was almost a certainty that he would run again the following year. If I ran, I would be a second candidate from Region
II — a big protocol taboo. So, I had to wait, but I didn't plan to
sit on my laurels.

When I returned to San Diego from Milwaukee, my daughter was nearing her pregnancy due date. I noticed that the September horoscope for Taurus in the San Diego Union-Tribune's
"By the Stars" column mentioned the possibility that someone
might be "leaving or entering the family circle." By the end of
the month, I would mark this up as one of those times when
horoscope generalities seemed a perfect fit. We welcomed that
little someone "entering the family" with much jubilation
when Cheryl gave birth to Shauna Pallas Sonnenwald — the
most beautiful baby ever, as seen through my first-time grandmother's eyes. I was so pleased when Cheryl honored me with
the baby's middle name. Cheryl knew that in later years, I
wished I had kept my maiden name as my middle name when
I began my career — and now my granddaughter would have
that middle name.

Just six days after Shauna's birth, we said a final goodbye to
Naudine as she "left the family circle" in her 87th year. John was
an only child, so after his death, I was Naudine's closest relative

Proud "Ahma" with first grandchild, Shauna Pallas Sonnenwald.

and I looked after her in John's stead. Although Naudine never lived with me, she spent a lot of time with our family and we would all miss her. It seemed especially fitting that my September horoscope should foretell Naudine's departure since she was an avid follower who liked to call my attention to the "Stars" column. Although our family experienced joy and sorrow that fall, my responsibilities outside the circle continued.

I volunteered to be chairman for the visit of our International President, Pat Panfile and his wife, Julie, scheduled for early November. As chairman for this special event, I was responsible for the entire stay of our guests. This included scheduling radio and television appearances, arranging speaking engagements with civic organizations and meetings with corporate executives in the San Diego area. Of course, the object of all these appearances, interviews and meetings was to promote Toastmasters and explore new club possibilities.

I soon realized that I had volunteered for a demanding and frustrating job that required numerous telephone calls and a vigorous letter writing campaign. Most contacts had to be made more than once — CEOs and corporate executives gave their own schedules priority and TV stations were reluctant to commit to a firm time for an interview. Allowances for driving time between appointments had to be included in the schedule and San Diego traffic flow could be unpredictable. Any last minute changes were likely to affect the entire agenda. Needless to say, I found this to be one hectic task!

On the big day, Mary English and Laura Stubbs escorted our First Lady, Julie, on a San Diego sightseeing and shopping tour while District Governor Les Stubbs and I accompanied the President on his appointed rounds. With a few minor adjustments we navigated San Diego traffic without any unexpected delays. We made our appointments on time and returned to the Sheraton Hotel on Harbor Island where the Panfiles reunited for a brief respite before attending the cocktail party Friday evening. On Saturday, I could relax a little. President Panfile spent the day at the District 5 Conference with time set aside for a chat with San Diego Mayor Pete Wilson. My duty as chairman of the President's visit ended the next morning with Julie and Pat Panfile on their way to the airport. With this task complete, I began to think of ways to keep myself active, useful and visible until I could officially begin my campaign for 3rd Vice President.

The holiday season arrived with the usual round of events including the Parade of Lights party at my condo and our family gathering. It was three-month-old Shauna's first Christmas. However, another event put me in the spotlight that year — the Center's Christmas party at the famed Hotel Del Coronado. I was front and center as master of ceremonies, and I had a superb evening. I had come some distance and was forging new memories in the same beautiful spot that held sweet memories of my special celebration with John.

After the first of the year, I kept active in Toastmasters in the role of district advisor and spent most of my weekends attending events in Region II. When summer came, I attended two large events in Phoenix, Arizona. The first event was the National Speakers Association (NSA) Convention at the Arizona Biltmore where I met NSA's founder, Cavett Robert, who was also a Toastmaster. At this time, NSA membership stood at 1500 and included a number of professional speakers; some very famous people graced that convention floor. I spotted Art Linkletter from a distance. At that time, I couldn't even imagine that someday he and I would stand face to face and I would be the one to place Toastmasters' highest honorary award, the Golden Gavel, in his hand.

A few weeks later, I was back into the Phoenix heat to attend the Toastmasters 50th International Convention at the Hyatt Regency. Appropriate to the occasion, one of our old timers and my good friend, Dr. Millard Bennett, delivered the Convention keynote address. At 87, he was dynamic and inspirational. This year marked another new experience for me — I attended the Past International Officers and Director's Luncheon where I was the first woman eligible to enter the realm of these distinguished Toastmasters.

I had waited a year for the outcome of that year's election and the news was good. When John Latin was elected 3rd Vice President, the door opened for me! We had anticipated his victory and passed out "HELEN — 82" campaign buttons to launch my campaign as the Convention ended. I was on my way at last!

Chapter 13

The Road to the Top

Though I would be the first woman to tackle this challenge, the path to the top was well worn and I never thought of myself as a trailblazer. Others may have seen my gender as significant, but I knew I was a Toastmaster who had earned her place in the organization's leadership and would follow the exact path that all others followed in pursuit of this office.

Nonetheless, I saw one obstacle in my path that kept me unsure of the outcome. Would the organization be willing to elect another 3rd Vice President from Region II? The year ahead would tell, of course. Meanwhile, there was work to do and I was eager to begin.

As I began to plan my strategy, I consulted my advisors, Ken Himes, the "swan song" conference chairman, and Bob Bolam, my important mentor since the days of Homer. We agreed that our first priority would be to make a good showing in the opinion poll. I went to work immediately, making calls and sending letters to all the eligible voters: members of the International Board of Directors, Past International Directors for the previous two years, Past International Presidents, district governors and immediate past district governors. Each of these officials is allowed to vote for up to two candidates. The nominating committee uses the outcome of the opinion poll as a guide in selecting the two candidates they present to the voters at the International Convention. (People can run from the floor if they wish but the nominating committee candidates have the advantage.)

When the opinion poll results were announced, I received 75 votes and Ted Wood from Region VII — Northeastern United States — received 44. This was a boost to my campaign but certainly not conclusive. I was off to a good start, though the nominating committee was not bound by the results of the poll and anything could happen.

Then one day, Past President "Dobbie" Dobson, head of the nominating committee called, and my heart began to pound.

He asked, "Would you accept the nomination for 3rd Vice President?"

What a question — *Would I?*

"Yes, indeed!"

When my feet touched Earth again, I heard the cautionary whisper of reality. A tough campaign still lay ahead. I was one of the two official candidates and Ted Wood was a very worthy opponent: competent, well qualified and personable. My campaign would now shift away from the poll of Toastmasters leadership and focus on other influential Toastmasters, including the district governors who would be carrying their club proxies to the Convention.

This portion of my campaign included visiting Region II districts in the spring and traveling to as many regional conferences as possible in June. My campaign chairman, Ken Himes, worked out a schedule with me for the months leading up to the August Convention. Two regional conferences are scheduled for each weekend in June. I couldn't attend them all, so we put Vancouver, New Orleans, St. Paul and Toledo on my June calendar.

Since all my campaign trips, including regional conferences and the International Convention, were at my own expense, I could take extra days and side trips. I sometimes made a stopover in Nebraska when Dad was still with us.

During one of our father-daughter chats, he said to me, "Honey, when you get this job that you want so badly, how much money will you make?"

I'll never forget the look of utter disbelief I saw on his face as I happily told him that the salary would be "absolutely nothing."

This return on my investment of time and money did not seem rational to a man who had struggled to raise five children during the depression years. However, I have always considered myself well paid for my Toastmasters effort. In fact, the value of all I have received from the organization is priceless.

Given that Region V's conference wasn't on my June schedule, I kicked off my campaign tour with that region's midwinter governor's conference in Chicago. I stayed with Milt and his family in Waukegan and borrowed his car to drive into Chicago for the event.

Since I was born and raised in Nebraska, I am familiar with Midwest winters. However, the weather that weekend was the worst I had ever seen. The Chicago Tribune headline for January 11, 1982 read "THE COLDEST DAY OF THE CENTURY" and reported an official temperature of 26 degrees below zero with a wind chill factor of minus 90 degrees.

Even so, I made contact with many Region V governors and had a chance to visit with my good friend, Past International Director Dick Storer. Bob Bolam had introduced me to Dick in

1974 at the International Convention in Anaheim. That had been my first Convention when I was campaigning for Durwood English in his run for 3rd Vice President. Connecting with old friends is always an enjoyable part of Toastmasters events, and this conference was worth the venture into an arctic zone. Though there had been occasions in my life when I had been apprehensive about some situations — such as staying in an all-male Navy BOQ — driving in this weather alone to see Region V leaders felt less daunting. Perhaps it was simply that I had grown more confident in my ability to handle tough situations.

After returning to San Diego, I visited as many Region II districts as possible. Then my visits to regional conferences began. Some regions invite international candidates (Director and 3rd Vice President) to question and answer caucus sessions.

As I moved from one room to another at one of these caucuses, I overheard a disparaging remark about women in leadership positions. Loudly spoken as I came near, the remark was clearly a message for me. I told my escort that I found the remark distressing and added, "I thought this chauvinistic attitude was old history."

I have never forgotten his reply, "Helen, if you can't stand the heat, you'd better get back in the kitchen."

I had to smile; I definitely had an advantage here. Based on the popularity of my gourmet dinners among the Toastmasters in San Diego, I figured that I could handle both the kitchen and the heat about women in leadership positions. Soon after that, a number of influential people put their support for me in writing. All the districts within our region issued proclamations bearing the officers' signatures and I received letters from the captain at the Center and San Diego Mayor Pete Wilson.

August came and I was ready for the history-making event that would take place at the International Convention in Philadelphia that year. And what history! Toastmasters International was about to add to the long legacy of this city — a place that held deep memories of the founding of a nation that has always strived for the equality of its citizens. The results of this election would determine whether Toastmasters would have its first black or first female 3rd Vice President. One of us would be on the road to the presidency. Later, when the United States began its process for the 2008 presidential election, and was facing a similar situation, I could view it with the perspective of one who had been there.

A few days before the Convention, my son Bruce and I boarded a plane for Philadelphia. We had a stop in Phoenix where I noticed Art Nieto and other District 3 Toastmasters coming aboard. Just knowing these staunch supporters were bound for Philadelphia with me raised my morale a notch. We would march on the Convention together.

We arrived on Saturday evening. The Convention was due to open on Wednesday. With several long days of campaigning ahead, I tried to protect my feet by staying on carpeted areas while we greeted early arrivals. Of course, I invited them to drop by my hospitality room to relax and enjoy our ever-popular margaritas.

Bruce had joined Toastmasters, and he was a great campaigner — women enjoyed talking to a single tall man. He was easy to spot in the crowd and served as a 6'6" beacon that drew people to me. Bruce was good for my campaign as a supportive Toastmaster and close relative. Family support was important to many Toastmasters and my son's presence would certainly capture a few votes.

Courtesy Toastmasters International

Bruce and I campaigning for 3rd Vice President at the International Convention in Philadelphia in 1982. I won this election

Finally, Wednesday arrived and we were busily campaigning in the lobby when I realized that the opening ceremonies were about to begin. Bruce and I made a dash for the escalator.

As we neared the top, a WHQ staff member greeted us with, "Thank goodness you're here! We're about to start!" Then, to my astonishment, he told me that I was on the program to give the invocation.

In the flurry of the campaign, I hadn't taken time to look at the program. My mind went blank, and all I could think of was to call for a minute of silent prayer. Then, I caught a glimpse of the man who could help, Don Ensch from District 33. I had known Don for some time and remembered that he was a devout Catholic who had considered the priesthood at one time. Certainly, he could come up with some powerful words that would inspire the crowd. Upon hearing my dilemma, he jotted down a quick prayer that saved the day for me.

Another longtime friend came through for me the next day. Back then, in the grand finale of the campaign, seconding speakers introduced each candidate and presented his or her qualifications to the voting body. The ideal seconding speaker was a strong supporter, well known and respected in the international community. And of course, it would be someone who wanted the candidate to win. I chose my good friend, Past International Director Dick Storer from Illinois to speak on my behalf. No one could have done a better job. Still, I felt uncomfortable as I stood on stage listening to Dick speak. His words made me feel proud yet humbled me at the same time. Later, I would learn the sacrifice he made to be there for me.

As it turned out, Dick and his wife, Charlotte, went far beyond my expectations. While they vacationed along the way to Philadelphia, Charlotte developed a kidney stone problem. After receiving medical advice, they decided to fly back to Chicago for her treatment. With surgery likely to take place on Saturday, Charlotte insisted that Dick keep his appointment at the Convention. She felt sure that he could deliver his seconding speech in Philadelphia on Thursday and be back in Chicago before her surgery. That is what he did. I am not sure there is ever a way to thank friends like these, except perhaps to pay it forward. Whenever I'm called on to help a friend, I think of what Dick and Charlotte did for me. Then, I step forward and help in any way I can.

After the votes were counted, the results were posted, and projected onto a large screen. The room fell silent as the names and numbers appeared. I held my breath for a moment. Suddenly, there it was — I won!

This was one of the happiest times of my life. We were just ecstatic — all of us — my son, my campaign team, my supporters at the Convention and me. After the excitement settled a bit, my opponent and I worked our way through the crowd for a friendly exchange. Ted congratulated me and I encouraged him to run again. I sincerely hoped that we would work together on the Executive Committee in future years, and of course, that came to be.

Bruce and I wore colonial costumes to the Colonial Block Party that evening. Of course, my election set the mood for our group and we could have had a great time anywhere. Nonetheless, it was an outstanding event with the Philadelphia Mummers and various street entertainers on the program.

I came to the Convention with a positive attitude, prepared to win, and I was ready to celebrate at the President's Dinner Dance on Friday night. I had worn black and white to blend in with the other directors when I was installed as International Director in 1978. This time, as 3rd Vice President, I no longer felt the need to blend in. Women were part of the organization now. I wore the gown of my choice, and it was ... *bright red.*

Winning this election put me on the road to the top. When Toastmasters elect the 3rd Vice President, they are electing the person who will be groomed to become President in three years. If the 3rd Vice President performs as well as expected and continues to do so, that person will move up to 2nd Vice President, Senior Vice President and then International President. This process assures that every person who becomes President of Toastmasters International is well qualified and trained before taking office. There is an election for each Vice President and for the President so there is always the possibility of a challenge. In the history of the organization, however, only one person has been voted out after serving as 3rd Vice President.

Courtesy of Toastmasters International

The Executive Committee 1982-83.
Standing, left to right - WHQ Treasurer Don Smith, Second Vice President John Latin, Third Vice President Helen Blanchard, Executive Director Terry McCann.
Seated left to right - Past President William Hamilton, President William Miller, Senior Vice President Eddie Dunn

I returned to San Diego, to an avalanche of congratulations — cards, letters, and flowers were just pouring in. By this time, plans were underway for a celebration at my condo. We held an open house and more than 100 Toastmasters and friends dropped by to help me celebrate in person. Cheryl had a special t-shirt made for my granddaughter Shauna to wear, and she was the hit of the party.

The 3rd Vice President serves on the Executive Committee along with the 2nd Vice President, Senior Vice President, President, and Immediate Past President. My first year, the other members were John Latin, Eddie Dunn, Bill Miller and Bill Hamilton. Having served as an International Director, I knew the other Executive Committee members since we'd worked together before. So I felt quite comfortable at my first Executive Committee meeting.

Shauna was a hit at the open house celebration of my victory in Philadelphia.

During the annual November meeting, the Executive Committee plans the agenda for the February Board of Director's Meeting. The Executive Committee also formulates the organization's long-range plans. In addition to these responsibilities, each Vice President heads a standing committee of International Directors. The Senior Vice President heads the District Administration and Programming Committee. The 2nd Vice President heads the Education Committee, and the 3rd Vice President heads the Policy and Administration Review Committee. Leading these committees provides the experience and knowledge base necessary to serve as President. The Vice Presidents also serve as the presiding officers at regional conferences and conduct the training sessions at these events.

That first year, my duties included presiding at the Region IV Conference in Calgary, Alberta, Canada. It may have been the most memorable. The Saturday Fun Night was a western theme that included a bus ride to a ranch and a buffalo burger cookout. Along the way, masked bandits on horseback hijacked the bus.

Much to my surprise, the bandits hustled me off the bus and escorted me to a saddled pony. Oh, no! I hadn't been on a horse since my youth when I spent those long summer days herding cows away from that Nebraska cornfield. Although this was a riding pony and not a huge workhorse, I still had difficulty climbing in the saddle and I had to have help — much to the amusement of the passengers on the bus. But it was all in fun. I made the ride and the buffalo burgers were worth the effort.

At a banquet the following evening, I stretched the truth a little when I told the crowd, "I'm fine but the horse is still under the care of a veterinarian."

Blanchard Collection

At the Region IV Conference in Calgary, Alberta, Canada, masked "bandits" hijacked me off the bus and escorted me on horseback to the cookout at the ranch.

The next two years, I officiated at regional conferences in Arlington, Virginia; Montreal, Canada; Little Rock, Arkansas; and Austin, Texas. I have special memories of all these conferences and the many Toastmasters leaders and members I met during these visits.

In March of 1983, while I was looking forward to a steady climb up the Toastmasters leadership ladder, I suddenly became aware that I was vulnerable to a sharp decline in my career. The *powers-that-be* in Washington D.C. slashed the budget for the Data Bank operation. Despite letters from Command, the Applied Physics Laboratory in Seattle, and our FORACS office—the order held firm.

This unexpected and frightening turn of events abolished the Data Bank and my position! I was relieved to learn that all of the Data Bank personnel could find work in other departments.

However, my FORACS experience and Data Bank expertise fit a unique niche. Thus, as far as I could see, my future as a Federal employee looked grim. For almost a month, I didn't know whether I would stay at the Center or go. My FORACS experience seemed unlikely to qualify me for work outside the Center, though I found some solace in knowing that upper management was working on my behalf.

Nonetheless, the most positive encouragement came from the Taurus horoscope predictions that included these phrases: "added responsibility and recognition," "financial prospects brighter than originally planned," and "an apparent obstacle is merely a test." Sometimes, the Entertainment section of the newspaper can be entertaining and comforting!

To my surprise, my Toastmasters experience saved me! All those extra hours I spent preparing Better Briefing Workshops, Brown Bag Lunches and other projects related to better communication paid off. Command decided to create a staff position for me as Communications Specialist for the Center. For the next six months, I conducted seven workshops (graduating over 70 participants), assisted Center personnel in developing formal presentations, and evaluated briefings. I loved this work and hoped it would become a permanent position.

After six months, however, the captain detailed me to the Public Relations Department where I became Head of Visitor Information and Presentations. In this position, I coordinated the visits of high-level military officers and civilians to the Center. This included helping the guests connect with Center personnel, arranging transportation, scheduling briefings, reserving conference rooms and securing audiovisual equipment.

I was not enthusiastic about this assignment, at all. Nevertheless, this department was important to the Center and saying "No, thank you" to the captain would not be appropriate, especially when I needed a job. I supervised an outstanding five-person team and appreciated their skill and dedication.

We had a frantic schedule most of the time and managed several visits from high-ranking officials including the Secretary of the Navy. After Secretary of the Navy John Lehman's visit, I received a letter from Captain F. M. Pestorius expressing his "thanks and congratulations" to me and "my people."

About six months later, I received an Exemplary Achievement Award in "official recognition of outstanding performance" as Head of the Visitor Information and Presentations Office and a letter congratulating me for a "job well done." I appreciated this recognition, but after a year... I was ready to move on.

About that time, I heard of a vacancy announcement for the Head of the Technical Information Division (TID). I thought a college degree would be necessary and dismissed the thought of applying. Then, people started asking me if I had submitted my resume yet — some of these people were in higher-level positions. I kept thinking about applying; seesawing back and forth. It was a Navy-wide announcement — what chance did I have? Nevertheless, it was a potential promotion, and I was tempted. The Center had adopted a unique pay and classification system called the Demonstration Project. This combined my GS-12 with the GS-13 and labeled it DP-III. The potential promotion was to a DP-IV, which combined the standard GS-14 and GS-15. The promotion would depend on the assumption of additional responsibility and duties. With that in mind but without much hope, I submitted my qualifications — in two resumes. One focused on my Federal service background and the other detailed my experience in the Toastmasters Program.

A panel that made recommendations for the final decision reviewed the applications. Later, one panel member told me confidentially that they considered two outstanding applicants — both equally qualified. One, however, had outstanding Toastmasters experience. That was me, and I got the job! After so many good things had come into my life, I was in store for one more. I would soon sit behind the desk in that corner office where we had taped the FORACS video — the office I had so admired. Now, it was my office, and I would be able to enjoy that unobstructed view of the Bay and the Pacific on our customary sunny and gorgeous Southern California days.

A month after I was elected Senior Vice President at the 1984 Toastmasters International Convention in Orlando, Florida, I assumed my duties as Head of the Technical Information Division. According to the job description, this Division's responsibilities included all technical reports, manuals, audiovisual, graphic arts products, photography and videos, plus two technical libraries and a branch in Hawaii. I had heard rumors of problems in this division and wanted to make my own evaluation.

As my first priority, I held a private meeting with each branch head to discuss needs and problems. Each meeting was more depressing than the one before it, and many evenings I went home wondering what I had gotten myself into. The branch heads reported low morale and discontent. They needed more people and updated equipment. To make this new job even more difficult, possible irregularities in attendance records called for a special investigation.

I saw a mountain of work ahead. Fortunately, there were many talented hard-working employees in the division, and I had support from top-level management. Although progress seemed slow, steps were taken to add personnel and modernize the equipment.

Throughout this eighteen-month period of job transitions, I continued an active role in the National Speakers Association — participating in workshops and conventions. As my schedule allowed, I accepted speaking invitations from an assortment of groups such as the Plastic Surgeons at Scripps Hospital, the Farm Bureau of Escondido, the Imperial Beach Lion's club, the Society for Technical Communication and the City Clerks of California.

As is the way of things, our family circle underwent change during this time. We lost my dear sister, Vlasta. Since my brothers, Bill and Earle, had already passed on, this left just two green shoots on Dad's branch of the Pallas family tree, Milt and me — the last of the five siblings. The Blanchard branch, however, experienced new growth. I gained a daughter-in-law when Bruce married Joanie in April 1984. Joanie and I bonded during the courtship and our relationship has grown over the years. I often tell people that if I could have handpicked a daughter-in-law, it would have been Joanie.

A highlight of my year as Senior Vice President was the privilege of attending the Service Club Leaders Conference at The Greenbrier, a luxury resort in West Virginia. Toastmasters Executive Director Terry McCann always took the Senior Vice President to this conference. Of course, this was the first year he took a woman. At that time, the major service organizations remained all male. The attendees included male leaders of men's organization, female leaders of women's organizations...and me.

I was the only woman there who was about to become president of a major former all-male organization. Throughout the weekend, I sat in meetings listening to presidents of the service clubs complain about declining membership and then vow to protect their all-male status. They continuously spoke of "the problem" saying that admitting "girls" would doom their chapters. The largest service organizations were especially vocal about their concerns. Many of them were facing legal action filed under antidiscrimination ordinances and laws in various states. Still, they insisted on continuing this futile battle to retain all-male memberships.

This was 1984; the Toastmasters organization had officially admitted women eleven years earlier. I have always been pleased that women became part of Toastmasters International without a legal battle. The leadership of the organization made a wise decision in allowing each club the option of being coed or all-male. Although some women disagreed, I saw no need to disturb those closed clubs at the time, and open membership did come about eventually. Nonetheless, I have always held a strong belief that women must have the opportunity to receive the valuable training Toastmasters provides.

Chapter 14

Madam President

1984 ended with the usual flurry of activity. However, there was no after-the-holiday slowdown for me in January. Toastmasters' first woman International President would take office in a few months and I had work to do. Finalizing my presidential theme topped my priority list. This theme would be the focus of my presidency and its legacy.

I took my time, giving it a lot of thought throughout my Vice Presidential years. I wanted to emphasize excellence in a meaningful message that would intensify the force of our great movement and offer lasting personal value to our members. I was influenced by Jeff Young's speech, "To Stand Before Kings," which took first place in the World Championship of Public Speaking at the 1980 International Convention. This speech carried the message that the stature of a person should not be measured by what they do but how well they do it. But I was still undecided and trying to work it out.

Then one day, John Stark, a good Toastmasters friend, carpooled with me to a Toastmasters event. He was about to take office as governor of District 5, and searching for a theme — for both of us — became a topic of our conversation during that drive. We found that we shared a desire to stress *excellence*. I don't remember who suggested the exact wording, but we agreed that "Commit to Excellence" would be a splendid theme for both of us. And so, this became his theme as governor and mine as International President.

My decision was reinforced by my personal belief that to get the best out of life, you must first get the best out of yourself. I was convinced that Toastmasters would grow and thrive if everyone would do every task well. From the smallest duty to the highest office, I wanted to encourage all Toastmasters to *Commit to Excellence*. Once the theme was decided, I had the foundation for my presidency in place.

Each incoming President presents a list of goals that they hope will be accomplished during their term. In keeping with my theme, I asked the districts to become "Distinguished Districts" and the clubs to maintain a membership of 20 and gain 3 new members during "my year" (1985-86). I also challenged each club to reach educational goals: two awards then known as Competent Toastmaster (CTM) and as Advanced Toastmaster (ATM) to be earned by their members. Last, but certainly not least, I wanted the organization to break the new club record. For several years, we had been trying to break the 500-club barrier and had almost succeeded in 1982-83 with 498 new charters. I desperately wanted to see that barrier broken.

In February, I presented my theme and goals for the coming year to my colleagues on the Executive Committee, the directors, and visitors attending the open Board Meeting. It was all received well. Thus, my Presidency was launched, and I could see no obstacles ahead. Yet, I was anxious for the election to be finalized and the introduction of Toastmasters International's "Madam President."

My Toastmasters schedule was light for the next few months, and I concentrated on my responsibilities at the Center. As the Center's well-known Toastmaster and experienced master of ceremonies, I was asked to organize and officiate at the retirement party for a department head who had enjoyed a long and distinguished career. Soon after that, I made a business trip to the Naval Weapons Center in China Lake, California. That spring, I conducted two technical workshops for our Center personnel.

On the family scene, we welcomed my second granddaughter, Elizabeth, into the family. The joy of her birth was clouded by concern. Soon after her arrival, this newborn underwent a blood change because of Rh factor incompatibility. She also had clubfeet. Correction of this birth defect included surgery on those tiny feet months before her first birthday, followed by more surgeries as she grew older. She took it all in stride and inspired us all with her remarkable attitude. Of course, my schedule included *grandmothering* these two little girls and supporting Cheryl during her daughter's surgeries.

By early summer, Toastmasters events filled my weekends and this heavy schedule would continue throughout my term as President. I had known this was coming, so I saved all the annual leave I could carry over from one year to the next. The normal work schedule at the Center was also a big help. As a part of an energy conservation/pollution reduction program, most of the Center's employees worked 9 hours 4 days a week, 8 hours one Friday with the next Friday off. Almost everyone loved a three-day weekend every other week, and it sure helped me stretch my annual leave to cover my Toastmasters travels.

June is regional conference month and my duties as Senior Vice President included serving as the presiding officer at the Region V Conference in Little Rock, Arkansas and the Region III

Blanchard Collection

On Christmas 1985, Elizabeth and Shauna are happy gals. Elizabeth is recovering from surgery and taking everything in stride, including casts on both feet.

Conference in Austin, Texas. I was also on the program at our Region II Conference in Irvine, California, where I led a panel discussion on leadership.

From July through mid-August, I barely had time to catch my breath. Preparing for the Convention included tasks for the outgoing Senior Vice President and preparations for the incoming International President. The Senior Vice President and chairman of the District Administration and Planning Committee had a report to prepare for the Board Meeting at the Convention. As the incoming President, I had an interview with an editor for an article in the Toastmaster magazine and a sitting for a formal portrait that would hang at WHQ throughout my term of office.

I also needed to prepare speeches for the Convention: one to district governors at the President's Breakfast and the other — the big one — my acceptance speech after the installation ceremony at the President's Dinner Dance. Experienced past presidents had told me to watch my speech time. One newly-elected President had been recorded in Toastmasters memory for a longer-than-necessary installation speech.

As one advisor so aptly put it, "They may not remember what you said, but they will all remember how long you spoke."

Remembering this, I prepared my speech with an eye on the clock, cut some material I had planned to use, and was able to complete my closing remarks in less than 20 minutes.

I also needed to plan the speeches I would deliver during my President's visits to a selection of districts. The governors of those chosen districts would review a list of my speech topics and choose which ones I would present at their district conferences. One of these speeches was about my theme, "Commit to Excellence," and the others were informative speeches containing a blend of educational and motivational material.

As the first woman International President, I wanted to look my best and present just the right image. For the top five officers, the three-day convention stretches to a week or more with before and after meetings and I needed a different outfit for each day and evening event. My carefully selected convention wardrobe included business suits, dressy outfits and a formal chiffon gown. By this time, I had learned that the Convention schedule leaves no time for a quandary over what to wear. So I made the wardrobe decisions before I packed, with an organized list of numbered items and pinned the corresponding numbers to each outfit and its accessories.

Those last few weeks were extremely busy, and the time rushed by. Mid-August arrived and I was ready for the 54th International

Convention at the Hyatt Regency in Columbus, Ohio. Attendance peaked with more than 1400 people that year, including
a large delegation from District 5 and most of my close family.
Bruce and Joanie accompanied me to Columbus. My stepmother
Irene, Milt and his wife, Florence, and their daughter-in-law,
Sandy, met us in Ohio. So did my niece, Dianne, and her husband, Dick. I was delighted to have these members of my family with me; they set aside time and made a long journey to be
there. Three-month-old Elizabeth was scheduled for surgery in
September, and so it was impossible for Cheryl to make the trip.
But I knew that she and the girls were with me in spirit.

The International Convention always had a packed schedule
with people rushing from one event to the next, crowding the
halls and elevators between sessions. It could become frantic at
times when the hotel was operating at maximum capacity. In
1985, however, only two of the four elevators were in service
and the glass elevator (outside the building) was inoperable
for one day. Creative rerouting helped most of us to assure
a timely arrival at our sessions. So, the audience understood
and loved it when I said, "This is the first time I took a 'down'
elevator to go up and the 'up' elevator to go down."

Nonetheless, it was a great Convention enjoyed by all.

The Columbus Police Color Guard and the Ohio State University Band led the opening ceremonies as they marched in
with the U.S. and Ohio State flags to stand at attention during
the National Anthem. Then, members bearing flags representing the nations that host Toastmasters clubs joined the parade
and circled the ballroom in a colorful and impressive display.
Next, Columbus Mayor Dana Rinehart and Ohio Governor
Richard Celeste welcomed us. This was followed by Toastmasters International President John Latin and Executive Director
Terry McCann presenting the status of the organization.

After this kick-off, the days of educational programs, meetings, Hall of Fame recognition and the Country Picnic Fun Night seemed to meld into a colorful blur. President Latin made the Golden Gavel presentation to Marva Collins, an educator known for her outstanding success in helping children with learning disabilities. Thursday finally arrived with the Annual Business Meeting and long-awaited election. According to parliamentary procedure, if there is only one candidate running for the office and other candidates have had ample opportunity to enter the race including a challenge from the floor, a motion to close the nominations with instruction to the secretary to cast a single vote for the single candidate is made and seconded. There had been no indication that a last-minute candidate might run from the floor.

However, the election wasn't over until the vote was cast and it was a huge thrill to hear the one vote cast by the secretary for "Helen Blanchard, International President!"

My heart pounded as the room burst into applause and cheering.

My first duty as President was a photo session where I shook hands with each of the 68 district governors. World Headquarters (WHQ) would distribute these photos in press releases to the governors' local newspapers, and the districts would place them in their newsletters. I started the ball rolling toward one of my goals for the year by taking a moment to personally ask each governor to lead his or her district to Distinguished District status.

As was usual in those days, the President's Dinner Dance and installation of officers and directors was held on Friday night. I wore a chiffon gown (with no lapel) which presented a dilemma for the pinning ceremony; however, John Latin solved the problem by piercing the corsage ribbon instead of the delicate fabric of my gown. This was the first time the incoming president was pinned on a corsage but I had a definite feeling that it wouldn't be the last. We also pinned incoming 3rd Vice President Tommy Richardson and welcomed him to the Executive Committee. The Committee now included: Senior Vice President Ted Wood, 2nd Vice President John Fauvel, and of course, Immediate Past President John Latin. I looked forward to working with these dedicated and capable members of the Executive Committee and the Board of Directors who would serve with me during my term as International President.

That night, as I took my place on stage to deliver my installation speech, I stepped into the spotlight and looked out at complete darkness; I couldn't see the audience at all. As I addressed my invisible listeners, I took the opportunity to thank the people who had encouraged me and participated in my campaign. I knew that Bob and Thelma Bolam, Dick and Charlotte Storer, and Durwood and Mary English were in the audience — so I had them stand while I thanked them for their advice and support. When I introduced my family, I couldn't resist tossing a playful jab toward my brother Milton.

I told my audience that after my defeat in Toronto eight years earlier, Milt had said, "Don't feel so bad, you're doing really well for a woman."

Then, after an appropriate pause, I added "Yeeees, I am!" The resounding laughter assured me that I had a large audience, out there, beyond the spotlight. It was an audience that understood just how far a woman could really go.

As I left the stage, I received a beautiful bouquet of roses from the Professional Men's Toastmasters Club in San Diego, congratulating me with a good-natured reminder that I still could not join their club because they had retained their all-male status. I

John Latin placed the President pin on the ribbon of my corsage instead of piercing the delicate fabric of my gown.

had been their area governor and enjoyed a good rapport with this group of dedicated Toastmasters.

I flew home to San Diego on Monday. The plane made a smooth landing, but my feet didn't touch ground for days. In the following weeks, a massive amount of mail arrived. I received congratulatory cards and letters from former Captains of the Center, U.S. Senator (California) Pete Wilson and other national, state, and city officials. I also received congratulations from many professional speakers in the National Speakers Association including the founder, Cavett Robert, past Toastmasters International Presidents, NATO friends, plus personal friends and co-workers. It was a heady time I will always cherish the memory.

In reality, I had to plant my feet firmly on the ground, I was still Helen Blanchard, a division head at the Center and Mom and Ahma (my granddaughters' name for me) at home. That

Board of Directors 1985-1986.

Bottom Row – (Left to Right)
Frank Chess (Secretary/Treasurer), John Fauvel (2nd VP), John Latin (Immedi-
ate Past President), Helen Blanchard (President), Ted Wood (Senior VP), Tom
Richardson (3rd VP), Terry McCann (Executive Director)
Second Row (Left to Right) International Directors
Jack Gillespie, Peter Crabtree, Jerry Starke, Mary Margaret Dockendorf, Anna
Frazier, Suzy Smith, Margaret Hope, Ted Randall, Louis Novak.
Top Row (Left to Right) International Directors
Joe Garmeson, Andy Anderson, James Seale, Henry Hyche, Howard Rivenson,
Herbert Nowlin, Les Stubbs, Frank Slane

September, I made a business trip to Hawaii to address some
problems with the branch office there and also made some
EEO presentations at the Center. On the home front, we celebrated Shauna's fourth birthday and I hovered at the hospital
while little Elizabeth underwent more surgery and Cheryl
spent long hours crib-side and worried.

Soon after arriving home, I received my agenda for the year
from Executive Director Terry McCann. I felt a little overwhelmed when I saw the travel schedule and considered my

other duties as International President. Terry McCann and his WHQ staff of about 40 people would oversee the day by day operations of our organization. As President, however, I was responsible for evaluating the performance of the WHQ operation including the approval and monitoring of the organization's budget. Other duties included approving Board expenses, chairing the Executive Committee, the Board of Directors, and the Long Range Planning Committee meetings. Along with other Presidents, serving before and after me, I cannot say enough about the dedication and capability of the WHQ staff. However, I was in touch with Terry McCann frequently for problems that did arise that needed my consideration.

At that time, each President visited one overseas district and my schedule included a visit to Johannesburg, South Africa. However, in the mid 1980s, the unrest — with racial violence and rioting in Johannesburg and the surrounding areas — constantly filled the headlines. As a result, it was decided that a Presidential visit to South Africa was unwise. It disappointed me that I would miss an overseas trip and a visit with our South African Toastmasters, but I was relieved that I would not be going into a highly-unstable area.

September melted into October and the beginning of my Presidential visits to the districts. That year, I made 11 official visits to districts during the fall and spring conference seasons. This included every weekend from October 10 through November 16 and April 10 through May 17. Throughout this time, I operated on a seven-day-a-week routine: fly to the conference city on Thursday, back to San Diego on Sunday, and work Monday, Tuesday and Wednesday at the Center. The following Thursday I was back at the airport.

My evenings in San Diego were spent writing "Thank You" notes, conferring with Terry, getting my clothes ready and packed for the next trip, tending to mail, and other details of my daily life (including paying bills and grocery shopping). Fortunately, I had studied (and given speeches) on time management and used all the tricks of the trade. Now and then, I envied the former presidents who had wives who assisted with many of these tasks. Nonetheless, I was always ready for the next visit and always made it to the airport on time.

Although each visit was unique, they all shared a common pattern. The district officers welcomed me at my destination and introduced me to the visit chairman who would keep me on schedule and chauffeur me on my appointed rounds.

The first evening, I met with the district leaders to get acquainted and go over the weekend schedule. This gathering ended early, allowing me some quiet time to settle in my hotel room and rest. Friday's appointments included meetings with corporation executives, military officials, university presidents, hospital administrators, state officials and mayors. Of course there was media coverage — with newspaper, television and radio interviews. Friday evening was usually set aside for socializing with district Toastmasters. During the Saturday conference, I always conducted an educational session during the day. I gave my "Commit to Excellence" speech that night, at the banquet, and usually had breakfast with the district leaders Sunday morning before my return to the airport and flight back to San Diego. Two of my visits (District 58 of South Carolina and District 36 of Washington D.C.) began a day early to accommodate the plans these districts had for me.

In the fall, I visited District 58 (South Carolina), District 22 (Kansas), District 54 (Illinois), District 39 (Northern California), District 18 (Maryland) and District 62 (Michigan). The spring visits included District 19 (Iowa), District 46 (New York

City), District 10 (Ohio), District 56 (Texas) and District 36 (Washington, D.C.).

These official district visits commanded 70 days and covered about 47,000 miles. I met with 34 corporate executives, visited 4 Government installations and 3 universities, received 16 proclamations from states and cities and the keys to eight cities. Overall, I felt like I had a red carpet rolled out before me as I traveled throughout this nation. I had a wonderful opportunity to promote the Toastmasters experience and enjoyed every moment of it.

Another opportunity came my way that I found personally fulfilling. I was invited to serve as a member of the 1985 National Awards Jury for the Freedoms Foundation, America's School for Citizenship Education. It was located in Valley Forge, Pennsylvania. The judging took place in November 1984 and required a few extra days annual leave between visits to Districts 18 and 62 (Maryland and Michigan). The 14 member jury included State Supreme Court Justices and leaders of educational institutes and service organizations.

During my four-day stay at this picturesque historical site, I helped judge the public communications entries in the national competition. I thoroughly enjoyed this once-in-a-lifetime experience and the occasion to honor good citizenship.

I had a lot of in-person contacts as International President, but media attention gave me the opportunity to reach out into the community in almost every city. I made appearances on 9 local television programs and 13 radio shows. I gave eight newspaper interviews. Some were brief spot announcements while others were in-depth interviews. Among the highlights: Paul Harvey told the "Homer story" on his syndicated radio show in August, 1985, and I made the Washington Post.

Throughout my term as International President, I received a
steady flow of articles clipped from the local news by Toastmasters across the country.

During my travels, I made a point to spend as much time as
possible talking to the individual members in each district. I
wanted to hear how involvement in the program affected daily
life so I asked hundreds of Toastmasters, "Has Toastmasters
helped you?"

They all had positive responses, and I was impressed when
I heard personal stories about the Toastmasters experience en-
hancing all aspects of everyday life. They were better employees, better managers, better family members and better citizens. They couldn't help but be more active in civic affairs.

As I traveled, I was pleased to see evidence that my theme,
"Commit to Excellence" had taken hold. Throughout the organization — from the club level to international — people were
putting forth their best effort. Of course, through the years of
Toastmasters history, our leaders had always been committed
to excellence; this was why we have such a great organization.
It's why our organization remains great to this day. Still, I felt
good about my theme choice — I wanted to encourage a commitment to excellence beginning with the smallest job at the
club level and reaching into personal lives.

All my visits were well-coordinated, extremely productive,
and ran smoothly on schedule. The coordinators for these
visits did a fantastic job. That's not to say everything was perfect. There were a couple of incidents that were extraordinary
and beyond the coordinators' control. One of these involved
a scheduled tenth television interview: four-minutes live on a
top-rated noon program. Much to my disappointment, President Reagan made a special speech to the nation that day. It
was broadcast live and preempted my interview. Later, during

my New York City visit, we became very aware that President Reagan was in Manhattan that Friday. The streets along his motorcade route were closed with police rerouting traffic at many intersections. Navigation was a nightmare but my dedicated coordinator made adjustments and we arrived at all the appointments on schedule. These close encounters with a United States President added to the experience and ultimately helped build some amazing memories.

In fact, this whole adventure was a delight, with many memorable highlights. My last official visit, Washington D.C., required an extra day. I especially enjoyed this visit since I worked for the Federal Government. I had lunch in the Senate Dining room and Senator Bob Dole, Republican Senate Majority Leader, joined us for an informal chat. I presented him with a Toastmasters Presidential Medallion and we shared a "photo op."

My appointment schedule included meetings with several other impressive Federal officials. The District of Columbia played a major role as well. Mayor Marion Barry Jr. gave me special recognition as the first woman President of Toastmasters International and issued a proclamation, making Thursday, May 15, 1986 "Helen M. Blanchard Day" in Washington, D.C. and I was presented a flag that flew over the Capitol on my birthday, May 17th. .

Over the years, I've treasured the memory of this personal touch that exceeded mere official recognition of my role as a visiting International President of Toastmasters.

My presidential duties extended beyond the district visits, of course. I presided over the Board Meetings in February and August. I concluded my official travels in June, serving at two Regional Conferences, Region I Conference in Salt Lake City, Utah and Region VIII in Mobile, Alabama. I also attended some

Blanchard Collection

During my last official visit, I presented Senator Bob Dole the Toastmasters Presidential Medallion in the Senate dining room.

local events in the San Diego area and took some time for the family (including a day at the circus with Shauna) before I began preparing for the grand finale and my presidential farewell.

This was scheduled for August, to take place at the International Convention at the MGM Grand Hotel, in Reno, Nevada.

Attendance at the Convention increased as the organization grew, and more than 2000 enthusiastic Toastmasters attended the 55th Toastmasters International Convention in 1986. The week I served as President at the International Convention may have been the busiest few days of my life. As President, I presided over the Board of Directors and other meetings that heralded the beginning of the Convention. While reporting the accomplishments of the year, I was pleased to announce that we had blasted through that 500 club barrier by establishing 552 new clubs.

Convention activities took every minute and I didn't miss any of it. I was so happy to share this glorious time with family and friends. Milt and Florence were there along with many dear friends from District 5... and all over the world. There were celebrity acquaintances among the attendees, as well. Patricia Fripp, the first woman President of the NSA gave the keynote address and Cavett Robert, the founder of that organization was in the audience.

As part of my official duties, I recognized our special guests and passed out the annual Toastmasters awards. I was pleased to give a President's citation to my mentor, Bob Bolam, and honored to give the Golden Gavel Award to TV personality Art Linkletter. As we chatted at the head table before the presentation, I allowed Mr. Linkletter to preview the award he would soon receive. He slipped the golden gavel out of its clear display case, and the handle almost fell off! We carefully positioned it back in its nest and he promised that he would leave the gavel in place when I presented it to him. In return, I quickly promised that Toastmasters would have it repaired for him post haste.

At the 1986 International Convention, I had the honor of presenting the Golden Gavel to Art Linkletter

As my last Presidential duty, I pinned Ted Wood, my successor and friend.

Our Thursday night Fun Night theme was "Hollywood Nostalgia" to go with the "Reach for the Stars" Convention theme. Many of the attendees came dressed as their favorite stars, and it was truly a sight to behold. Our most creative Toastmasters put their best talents on display in their effort to "go Hollywood."

The President's Dinner Dance and the installation of new officers for the coming year marked the end of my term. I had mixed feelings as I pinned Ted Wood, my successor and friend. Like a young girl at the prom, I didn't want the dance to end and I knew how John Latin felt when he said, "I ain't gonna go."

But there was also overwhelming joy; I was sure that I was placing the President's pin on the right lapel. Ted would take the helm of the Toastmasters program and "Keep the Spirit Alive," as his theme proclaimed. My year as President had ended, but my commitment to the program would go on.

Chapter 15

No Swan Song Yet

In August of 1986, I quietly slipped into a new position — Immediate Past President — and began my last year of service at the executive level. The following February, I received a scrapbook and the portrait that had graced the main lobby of WHQ during my year. Although I would serve as Immediate Past President until the 1987 International Convention, this February Board Meeting would be my last. I delivered my farewell speech to the Executive Committee and I was almost overcome with emotion when I said good-bye to this major part of my life.

All too soon, mid-August arrived again and I boarded a plane for Chicago and my last "official" Convention. That summer, Ted Wood, the outgoing President, passed the pin to John Fauvel who would preside as International President for the year, 1987-88. John was another first for Toastmasters, the third in a row after the first woman and the first minority. He lived in New Zealand and, hence, was the first International President who lived outside North America.

As Immediate Past President, I had the honor of being the master of ceremonies at the President's Dinner Dance. In the days leading up to the dinner, I watched for any interesting tidbits of news that I could use in my master of ceremonies comments. Sure enough, one tidbit developed that had caught everyone's attention.

We ate chicken at the luncheon the first day and it was on the menu every meal thereafter. By Thursday night, people were starting to mumble and by Friday evening, I was hearing complaints. Indeed, this was a situation that begged for some comment to ease the tension. So, during my opening remarks that night, I mentioned something about a book I thought would be of interest and suggested that they might find *425 Ways to Cook Chicken* on the hotel's newsstand. This brought the house down! After a dinner of beef steak that night, I asked how everyone enjoyed the dinner.

Of course, they responded with a hearty applause.

Then, I added, "If you look on page 52 of that book I mentioned, you will find a recipe for chicken that looks and tastes like beef steak."

My audience roared. Now and then, I meet a longtime friend at a convention who mentions the famous "chicken episode."

Although my Toastmasters International leadership role had ended, the years leading to my retirement in January, 1992, would be busy and rewarding. I stayed involved in my clubs, served as head of the advisory committee for several of our district governors and installed District 5 leaders. I spoke at local club installations and anniversaries and attended area and district events.

I traveled to Arizona twice during this period to be a guest speaker at District 3 Conferences. The regional conventions took me to Los Angles, Las Vegas and San Francisco — and I attended the International Conventions in Washington D.C. in 1988 and Palm Desert in 1989. I also accepted speaking invitations from organizations outside the Toastmasters community including the Navy League, the Medical Auxiliary, the San Diego Women's Club and the Tucson Chamber of Commerce.

As I recall the Toastmasters highlights of this time, the 1991 dedication of our new WHQ building in Rancho Santa Margarita, California, tops the list. In the thirty years since Dr. Smedley broke ground on the first WHQ site in Santa Ana, our membership had doubled and the organization had outgrown the original building. The Rancho Santa Margarita dedication was an elegant affair, complete with ribbon-cutting and speeches by Dr. Smedley's daughter, Executive Director Terry McCann, and other dignitaries. I was one of 23 past presidents to witness the unveiling of the granite wall bearing the names

Courtesy Toastmasters International

Our new WHQ building in Rancho Santa Margarita, California, dedicated in 1991.

of all who served and their years in office. This was the largest group of past presidents ever assembled in one place.

I was one of 23 past presidents attending the dedication and the unveiling of the granite wall bearing the names of all the past presidents and year in office.

Bottom Row - left to right -
Earl Potter (1968-69) - Joe Rinnert (1946-47) - Sheldon Hayden (1940-41) - John Haynes (1955-56) - Frank Spangler (1962-63) - Paul Haeberlin (1957-58) - John Miller (1966-67)

Top Row - left to right -
Ralph "Bud" Howland (1969-1970) - Arthur Diamond (1970-71) - John Diaz (1974-75) - George Scott (1975-76) - Bob Blakeley (1976-77) - Durwood English (1977-78) - H. E. "Dobby" Dobson (1978-79) - Pat Panfile (1980-81) - Bill Hamilton (1981-82) - Eddie Dunn (1983-84) - John Latin (1984-85) - Helen Blanchard (1985-86) - Ted Wood (1986-87) - John Fauvel (1987-88) - Tom Richardson (1988-89) - John Noonan (1989-90)

Meanwhile, at work I resumed my Center Presentation Workshops and conducted three per year for the next six years. My classrooms were always full. Many of the attendees were scientists and engineers who wanted to make better briefings to their colleagues, Command, and sponsors in Washington D.C. I was especially pleased when I reviewed the written evaluations and found flattering comments and assurance that the workshop participants appreciated my effort. The most significant comment came from Command, crediting my workshops with a definite improvement in the briefings given by Center employees.

A few months after I became Head of the Technical Information Division (TID) in 1984, plans were set in motion to rebuild morale, increase the workforce, and replace outmoded manual equipment with cutting-edge technology. An electronic documentation system was now in place to prepare the Center's reports and documents. Computer stations replaced light tables for the graphic artists and both technical libraries automated their collections. I was able to justify the need for more personnel and the division multiplied from 87 employees to a workforce of 133. Of course, the improved working conditions elevated morale, increasing performance and output. Before long, recognition came our way when a group from TID, including me, helped develop the Navy's first Program Management Training Course. The course proved to be successful and the project received the Navy Award of Merit.

About that time, I was promoted to a DP IV Grade Level (the equivalent of the GS-14/GS-15 rating) and I would retire at the GS-15 level. Thirty-one years had passed since I entered Government Service as a GS-3. In those early years, I advanced at a steady pace until I reached GS 12. At that time, the Personnel Department advised me that I could not advance any further and that my supervisors should not even apply. I thought I had reached the top in 1972 and was sure of it again in 1989. However, there was more to come.

In 1991, I received the highest honor the Center can bestow: the prestigious Lauritsen-Bennett Award, a prize named in honor of two gentlemen who made major scientific contributions to the Navy. Established in 1978, this award is given in recognition of excellence in three areas — engineering, science, and staff/support. I received this award for excellence in staff/support for "continuing and outstanding leadership of technical information functions" including the

Blanchard Collection

In 1991, I received the prestigious Lauritsen-Bennett Award. After attending the ceremony and reception at the Center, my family posed on top of Building 33 with beautiful San Diego Bay as the backdrop.

(Clockwise from the left - Joanie, Bruce, Cheryl, Helen, Elizabeth and Shauna.)

modernization of TID. According to an article in the Center's newsletter, one upgrade, the electronic documentation system "is estimated to have saved the Center $1,900,000 in the fiscal years 1988-1990." The other upgrades also improved our products and efficiency. As a result, the Center expressed gratitude for my "excellent support and dedication." Of course, I was most pleased to receive this honor and it doubly surprised me to learn that I was the first woman recipient. A formal presentation was held in the Center's auditorium followed by an informal reception at the Center's bayside recreation center, the Dolphin club. Again, congratulatory cards and letters came my way. One that touched me deeply was from a former Center Captain who credited my presentation workshops with helping to raise the quality of the Center's briefers to a level that could only be described as, "eloquent ambassador."

Once my evenings and weekends were no longer fully committed to Toastmasters, I had time to participate in more of the Center's social events. One summer, I took Shauna to the annual picnic at the Navy's Admiral Bakers Field. About the first attraction that caught her attention was the "dunk tank" with our technical director sitting in the "dunk seat." A dollar bought three soft balls and three chances to hit the target that would dunk the technical director. Eight-year-old Shauna begged for a chance. So of course, "Ahma" complied. To my amazement, that child had an arm and good aim. She hit the target — twice!

When the technical director climbed out of the water the second time, he asked, "Who is that little girl?"

"Helen Blanchard's granddaughter," came the quick reply.

I knew I would hear about this back at the Center. I did! Sometime Monday morning, Shauna became a celebrity.

Another activity that I thoroughly enjoyed took place in 1990 — a huge Chili Cook-off. Although I no longer gave those gourmet dinners, I had not lost my enthusiasm for cooking. I entered a big pot of black-bean chili. We had hi-level judges including the captain and the technical director. To my surprise, I won first prize — a blue ribbon and a sign that read "KILLER CHILI (best tasting)." Of course, I received many requests for the prize winning recipe. Unfortunately, I had made Brazilian Black Bean Feijoada from memory adding "a pinch of this" and "a little of that" until it tasted like "Killer Chili." I wanted to share the recipe so I made it again and measured everything. But I don't think it ever turned out the same.

During this time, I could again use my annual leave for vacationing and I took the big leap — a month long, cross-country driving tour, mostly alone. I headed east out of San Diego and picked up my niece, Ruthann Stevens in Tucson. We shared driving to Nebraska where we visited family. Then she returned to Tucson and I drove on to Waukegan to see Milt and his family. From the Chicago area, I wandered along a scenic route back to San Diego through South Dakota's Black Hills, Wyoming, Colorado and Arizona. As I headed back to San Diego, I took a detour to enjoy one of Arizona's most picturesque drives through Oak Creek Canyon and Sedona. I rented a cabin, stayed in Oak Creek Canyon a few days, and reminisced about my family's visit twenty years earlier with John and the kids.

In all my travels, I very rarely felt uncomfortable about driving alone. I learned to be cautious and plan ahead. I chose Holiday Inn-type motels located in the midst of populated areas along the main road. I always started driving early in the day and checked in for the night by mid-afternoon. I asked motel personnel for restaurant recommendations and directions. Then, I enjoyed the local fare and settled into my room before nightfall. On the rare occasion that I felt uncomfortable, I would say, "My husband is nearby waiting for me."

Shortly after I celebrated my 65th birthday, I set the date of January 3rd, 1992 to end my 33 year career in Federal Service. The Dolphin Club was the site of yet another celebration — this time with old friends and family, employees, colleagues and supervisors. I parted with pangs of sadness mixed with bliss. I enjoyed my work, the people I worked with, and being a part of the workforce at the Center — but my heart had told me it was time to go. However, I was not planning to ride away quietly and fade into the sunset. True to my nature, I had plans.

I started a business that spring — Helen Blanchard Seminars — and presented, "The Winning Edge." I conducted my seminar a few times. But I soon decided that the work required for success — the marketing and all that went with it — just wasn't worth the effort for this retired lady. The experiment did, however, serve as a good transition to a complete and active retirement.

I set a new agenda for myself. The granddaughters and I made regular visits to the San Diego zoo, Sea World and the Wild Animal Park. I became more active in my church, working in the library and with Food Ministry. I started a walking program and accumulated over 2040 miles in the first three years. It seemed that the condo association had been counting the days until my retirement and they elected me president/treasurer. Since our association has no restrictive term limit regulations, I served in that position for the next 15 years.

With all these activities, I still found time for one of my favorite pastimes — travel. In 1990, I had taken an Alaskan cruise with

Milt and Florence, and also Trudy and Bob Martin — dear friends
I had known since John's Great Lakes Navy Training Station
days. We all enjoyed such a great time that I decided to celebrate
my retirement with a cruise of the Scandinavian Fjord lands on
the Queen Elizabeth 2 with the same cruise partners. We flew
to London to board the ship. Our ports of call, Stavanger and
Oslo, were the highlights for me. Visiting Stavanger, of course,
reminded me of my time there with the FORACS training group.
In Oslo, Katrina and Tor Berg, the good friends who shared my
FORACS memories, gave us a private tour of this lovely city followed by dinner in their beautiful home overlooking the harbor.
We enjoyed their gracious hospitality to the fullest.

Later, I cruised the Western Mediterranean with Bruce and
Joanie and the following year, we cruised the Eastern Mediterranean. During these travels, I stored away priceless memories of
the sights we saw and the fun I shared with friends and family.

I did not limit my European adventures to sea travel; I also
flew overseas continuing to fulfill that double crown prophesy. During my year as International President, I accumulated
frequent flyer miles and wanted to use them for Toastmasters
travel. I waited for a perfect opportunity and it came my way
in 1994 — the Continental Council of European Toastmasters
Conference in Vienna. What a thrill it was to meet Toastmasters from so many countries in Europe! I was honored to be a
guest speaker at the Conference.

From there, I went on to visit clubs in Munich and Prague. I
felt a special connection to Prague knowing that Dad had lived
near this city as a boy. I traveled to Prague on my own and rode
the train to Munich where I joined a tour of central Europe.

Though they called me brave to my face, I suspect my friends
thought I was foolish to set out on this European journey on
my own. I admit to being a little apprehensive since I only

speak English. However, I wouldn't hesitate to travel anywhere in Europe by rail — I found the trains comfortable, fast, on time, and felt perfectly safe.

While this visit to the European Toastmasters community was certainly a highlight of my retirement years, I enjoyed other events closer to home. In 2001, I attended the International Convention in Anaheim California. Twenty-seven years had passed since I attended my first convention there and many changes had taken place. JoAnna McWilliams presided over this Convention as International President, our third woman to hold this office following Pauline Shirley (1994-95), and me (1985-86). As I write this, our fourth woman president, Jana Barnhill is preparing to take the helm for the year 2008-2009.

As of 2007, three women had held the office of International President; Pauline Shirley (1994-1995), Helen Blanchard (1985-1986) and JoAnna McWilliams (2000-2001).

At the 2001 Convention, we bade farewell to our retiring Executive Director, Terry McCann, who had served the organization for 26 years. His invaluable leadership had guided our organization through major growth after the acceptance of women in our membership. During this time, Toastmasters International tripled in size, became financially secure, and earned a respected reputation for its educational program, worldwide. As Terry stepped aside, we welcomed another capable Executive Director, Donna Groh, who is guiding the organization through another major growth period as we expand internationally.

In my retirement years, I had more time to spend with family, I saw Milt and Florence often — they visited San Diego and I traveled to Waukegan. We vacationed together and celebrated their 60th wedding anniversary in 2000. Florence passed away in 2001 and Milt joined her eighteen months later. This left me the last of the Pallas Five. I feel blessed to have my son and daughter nearby and my granddaughters bring me such pleasure. Through the years I watched them race through childhood and adolescence and blossom into beautiful young women. We have enjoyed so many fun times and still do.

Our Christmas traditions changed through the years. The Data Bank group scattered and the Parade of Lights on San Diego Bay changed its route and no longer comes within close view from my balcony — so the viewing parties from my condo came to a halt. As the old traditions faded away, however, the growing family created new ones. In their youth, Shauna and Elizabeth took charge of decorating my patio; stringing lights and checking each bulb, preparing my condo for Christmas Eve. Through the years, Christmas Eve has always remained a family time with gifts exchanged after a ham buffet dinner. The location may vary but the love and fun is always present.

One Christmas we abandoned all tradition as we kept vigil over an ill child. Eight-year-old Elizabeth was in Children's Hospital awaiting surgery to remove an aneurism deep in her brain. This was a very frightening time for us all. Elizabeth, of course, looked forward to Santa's visit and wanted to be at Ahma's on Christmas Eve. Since this was impossible, the hospital allowed us to celebrate Christmas in her room. We trooped in with gifts, a ham and trimmings, and the most upbeat holiday spirit we could muster. Elizabeth's successful surgery took place a few days later and we will always be grateful to the skilled surgeon and the wonderful staff at Children's Hospital for their care and compassion during this difficult time.

The years flew by. My family and I experienced the triumphs and defeat, ills and recoveries that meld into the cycle of life. January of 2000 arrived to herald the new millennium and the years continued their flight. In May 2006, my two nieces, Ruthann Stevens and Dianne Barbour, joined me when I was the featured speaker at our District 5 Conference.

My nieces, Ruthann Stevens and Dianne Barbour, joined me when I was the featured speaker at our District 5 Conference, in May 2006.

This Conference celebrated my 20th Anniversary as the first woman President of Toastmasters International. That same month, I passed another milestone — my 80th birthday celebration. How did this happen so quickly? Suddenly, I am an octogenarian. It has been a great eighty years, and I can't wait to see what happens next — every time I think my swan song is about to be sung, a new tune fills the air, instead.

The District 5 Conference celebrated my 20th Anniversary as the first woman President of Toastmasters International. About that same time, I passed another milestone – my 80th birthday.

Chapter 16

Reflections

Looking back at my life experiences, a common thread seems to be woven in the tapestry of my years. From my Nebraska school teaching days, to success in Federal Service, then attaining the highest office in Toastmasters, I accepted challenges that made me reach far beyond my comfort zone, time and again.

Some people say, "You were in the right place, at the right time."

I was — and I credit Toastmasters for training that gave me the confidence and communication skills to pursue the opportunities that came my way. Toastmasters also gave me the knowledge -- information that I could teach in workshops at the Center. Ultimately, my ability to share this knowledge earned me recognition and more opportunities.

This is not to say that I didn't work hard every step of the way. I did. There were many times that I went the extra mile on my own time; I have spent countless evenings and weekends of my life preparing myself for the challenges ahead. Through all that effort, I earned the confidence of my supervisors, and they considered me for promotions based on merit.

I entered the workforce at 16 years of age. My working and active retirement days span more than sixty years and bridge two centuries. And in that time, I have seen a lot of change. When I applied for my first job, few women hoped for anything beyond becoming a wife and mother. In my generation, single women and wives who worked outside the home could be receptionists, store clerks, secretaries and bookkeepers. Although there were a few female doctors and lawyers, most professional women were nurses and teachers.

After a long struggle, women had won the right to vote in 1920 and the effort to gain equal rights continued at a slow but persistent pace. By the time I retired in 1992, a great amount of progress had been made. Women were welcome in every service organization in America and some were serving as corporate CEOs. Women occupied seats in the U.S. House and Senate, Geraldine Ferraro won the nomination as the Democratic candidate for Vice President of the United States six years earlier, and another woman with presidential aspirations of her own "took office" as first lady that year.

After a recent speech about my Toastmasters experiences, a young female Toastmaster came up to me and thanked me for "battering down that Toastmasters door."

I quickly responded, "I didn't batter down any doors. I came in through the side door and helped the men open the front door for all of us." I know that I was fortunate to be surrounded by open-minded people who supported my efforts. At least, those in my club were supportive and that was all it took for me to continue and ultimately prove myself to those who questioned the capabilities of women.

J. Clark Chamberlain, the principal organizer and first International President, strongly opposed allowing women in Toastmasters from the beginning and for several years thereafter. I will always treasure the letter I received from him in 1977. "What you have done for us...during your entire career as a Toastmaster, certainly changed my views," he wrote. "Women Members are a reality, and their numbers are increasing rapidly. They are entitled to representation, surely, and you are the one to "break the Ice."

I was in the workforce as equal rights slowly blossomed into reality. Perhaps it was a combination of efforts — of the women who actively protested, and the women like me who proved our worth daily, on the job. I also helped make opportunities available and recommended deserving women for advancement through the EEO, Upward Mobility, and Federally Employed Women programs. These avenues were available to me and participating in them fit "my way." I will always be grateful to those who came before, who helped develop the notion of women's equality in this country, so that the Federal government would have these programs available for my benefit...and for the benefit of those deserving women I assisted, in turn.

I've had opportunities, enjoyed many benefits, and I'm proud to have participated to the fullest — in life, on the job, and in Toastmasters. This program changes lives because you will never stop learning; growing; and becoming the best person you can possibly be. After nearly 40 years of continuous membership, I still attend club meetings regularly; enjoy speaking engagements and welcome invitations. When people ask me why, my answer is always the same: When you get out of Toastmasters all you can get out of Toastmasters...you'll never get out of Toastmasters!

This is the avenue still open for me to encourage others on their journey. This practice has always been rewarding to me and has a hidden benefit. What is it? I have a plaque in my study that says it best — "When you help someone up the hill, you find yourself closer to the top."

About the Authors

Helen Blanchard, a Nebraska cornhusker by birth, now resides in Point Loma, a seaside neighborhood of San Diego, California. She is retired from a successful career at the Navy's research and development center after 33 years of federal service. Her Toastmasters career went from "Homer" (the name given her in the all-male organization) to Madam President. She is listed in *Who's Who of American Women*, *World Who's Who of Women*, and *International Learders in Achievement*.

Deanne Durrett is the author of 20 nonfiction books for kids, mostly at the junior high and high school level, plus almost 200 newspaper and magazine articles and stories. *Breaking the Ice* is her second ghostwritten book and she has enjoyed this stroll down Helen M. Blanchard's memory lane. Deanne Durrett has lived most of her life in San Diego but returned to her home state of Oklahoma in 2005, where she lives with her husband, Dan, and two cats. She has family nearby and enjoys the season change and weather. To learn more about this author, please visit her web site, http;//www.deannedurrett.com.